STARTING OUT QUICKLY WITH

Microsoft Visual C++

Doug White

University of Northern Colorado

Scott/Jones, Inc.
P.O. Box 696
El Granada, California 94018
Voice: 650-726-2436
Facsimile: 650-726-4693
E-mail: marketing@scottjonespub.com
Web page: //www.scottjonespub.com

ISBN: 1-57676-133-9

Starting Out Quickly with Visual C++ .NET by Doug White, University of Northern Colorado

ZYX   543

ISBN: 1-57676-133-9

The publisher wishes to acknowledge the memory and influence of James F. Leisy. Thanks, Jim. We miss you.

Text Design: Cecelia G. Morales
Cover Design: Nicole Clayton, Design Graphx, and Joshua Faigen
Copyediting: Heather Moehn
Composition: Amnet Systems Private Limited
Proofreading: Kristin Furino, Holbrook Communications
Book Manufacturing: WebCom
Printed in Canada

Scott/Jones Publishing Company
Editorial Group: Richard Jones, Denise Simon, Leata Holloway, and Patricia Miyaki
Production Management: Audrey Anderson
Marketing and Sales: Victoria Judy, Page Mead, Hazel Dunlap, Donna Cross
Business Operations: Michelle Robelet, Cathy Glenn, Natascha Hoffmeyer, and Bill Overfelt

A Word About Trademarks
All product names identified in this book are trademarks or registered trademarks of their respective companies. We have used the names in an editorial fashion only, and to the benefit of the trademark owner, with no intention of infringing the trademark.

Additional Titles of Interest from Scott/Jones

Computing with Java™: Programs, Objects, Graphics,
Second Edition and Second Alternate Edition
From Objects to Components with the Java™ Platform
Advanced Java™ Internet Applications, Second Edition
    by Art Gittleman

Developing Web Applications with Active Server Pages
    by Thom Luce

Starting Out with Visual Basic
Standard Version of Starting Out with C++, Third Edition
Brief Version of Starting Out with C++, Third Edition
    by Tony Gaddis

Starting Out with C++, Third Alternate Edition
    by Tony Gaddis, Judy Walters, and Godfrey Muganda

C by Discovery, Third Edition
    by L.S. and Dusty Foster

Assembly Language for the IBM PC Family, Third Edition
    by William Jones

QuickStart to JavaScript
QuickStart to DOS for Windows 9X
    by Forest Lin

Advanced Visual Basic. NET, Third Edition
    by Kip Irvine

HTML for Web Developers
Server-Side Programming for Web Developers
    by John Avila

The Complete A+ Guide to PC Repair
The Complete Computer Repair Textbook, Third Edition
    by Cheryl Schmidt

Windows 2000 Professional Step-by-Step
Windows XP Professional Step-by-Step
    by Leslie Hardin and Deborah Tice

The Windows 2000 Professional Textbook
The Visual Basic 6 Coursebook, Fourth Edition
Prelude to Programming: Concepts and Design
The Windows XP Textbook
    by Stewart Venit

The Windows 2000 Server Lab Manual
    by Gerard Morris

Acknowledgements

Dedicated to Vicki and Katie for allowing me the time to write this book without complaint. I would also like to thank Audrey Anderson and Richard Jones for making the book happen at all and, of course, my students who always put up with the drafts and misprints.

Contents

1

Introduction to Compilers

The world of technology is an exciting and dynamic place. All of the players must constantly work to maintain and upgrade their skills if they wish to remain viable in the technology field. This book is directed towards students of programming who wish to get a quick overview of how to use Microsoft's Visual C++ .NET Edition to accomplish their programming goals.

This book will assist you with using the technology, but it is not designed to teach you how to program in Visual C++. The book covers a variety of topics including:

- Working with projects and workspaces
- Creating C++ files
- Compiling
- Debugging source code for both syntax and logic errors
- Creating different file types in Visual C++ .NET
- Getting started using Visual C++ .NET quickly with tutorials

Overview of Compilers

In programming, a compiler is a tool, an engine that works on your behalf to process instructions and allow you to deal with the various components that make up a computer. The compiler's job is to make sure you follow the basic rules of the language, and if you make up new rules, to provide enough information so the compiler can translate your instructions into language the components can understand.

Thus, a compiler traces the following set of steps:

List 1.1

1. Get the set of instructions from you.
2. Review the instructions to see if any violate the rules.
3. If all the rules are obeyed, create a working file in the language of the computer (machine language).

4. Attach to the working file full instructions for any shortcuts you may have used.
5. Assemble a final file in machine language.

Example 1.1

Suppose you have a robot that can manufacture just about anything if you write a set of instructions. You decide to try to have the robot manufacture a cheeseburger. Many of the components can simply be described by name and the robot will know what you want. So, you write the following instructions:

Take a bun and split it in half.
Take a one-quarter pound ground beef patty.
Take a slice of cheddar cheese.
Cook ground beef patty until the internal temperature is 130 degrees.
Place ground beef patty on bottom of bun.
Place cheese on ground beef patty.
Place top of bun on cheese.

Most humans could follow these instructions, but the robot needs specific instructions. Since you don't want to instruct the robot every time some common actions occur, such as "cook" or "take," these actions might be included in a library of common actions that come with the robot. A great many common actions (often referred to as ANSI standards) are included with the C++ compiler you are using. These instructions are included with Visual C++ and are called a library or header file. Thus, the compiler will take your instructions and make sure you haven't used terms that aren't defined (for example, secret sauce for the cheeseburger). If you have used undefined terms, it will ask you to define them, do away with them, or change them in order to work with the compiler. Any terms that the compiler understands can then be associated with the complex instructions needed to accomplish the task. This type of operation will save you a lot of time since you can simply say "cook" instead of providing a full explanation of how to cook each time it comes up.

Compiler Files

Every compiler uses a set of files to perform its operations. There are four main files that exist on most compilers for almost every programming language:

- The source code
- The object file
- The linked/library file
- The executable file

The Source Code

Source code is the heart of any program. It is the set of instructions that you will develop on your own for processing by the compiler. Source codes on Intel-based platforms are often developed in ASCII.

Definition 1.1

ASCII refers to the American Standard Code for Information Interchange, a system of encoding letters, numbers, and symbols (e.g., ∞) into a set of 8-bit binary numbers. This system is used by all the Intel-based PCs and is common throughout the world. Many foreign character sets have also been added into the ASCII set. The most common terminology for this is DOS TEXT or TEXT files.

Figure 1.1
The C++
Source Code
Icon

ASCII files can be created with just about any word processor or simple text editors such as Notepad. Many modern compilers attempt to go beyond this approach and incorporate their own environments for developing source code.

In Visual C++, the source code files have an extension to make them easy for you (and the system) to identify. The extension is **.cpp**. This extension on a filename (e.g., **myProg.cpp**) tells the programmer that this is a C++ source code file, and it tells Microsoft Windows-based operating systems to use the Visual C++ editor to manipulate the file. These files usually associate with an icon that looks like Figure 1.1.

You should always adhere to the standards for files of a given type as this will help you locate the files later and make sure that your compiler is able to interpret them correctly. Visual C++ may mishandle C++ programs that do not have the **.cpp** extension. If you use Visual C++ to create the source code files, they will have this extension by default.

The Object File

Object files are created by the compiler and often have the extension **.obj**. These are files that have been processed through the first series of steps by the compiler (steps 1 and 2 in List 1.1). The files contain the source code that you have created, but now the source code has been converted into machine language and the file is no longer readable by you. **NOTE:** If step 2 is not completed successfully (i.e., you have broken some of the rules of the compiler), the object file will not be created and you will not be able to proceed until you have overcome the problems. This process is called **debugging**.

Definition 1.2

Debugging is the process of removing errors from the source code. It typically comes in two types: syntax debugging and logic debugging. Syntax debugging is working to get your source code into a form the compiler will accept. Logic debugging is testing to determine if errors in programming are creating errors in output even though the program instructions adhere to the rules of syntax.

The Library File

When an object file is created, the compiler must also create a **library file** of instructions. These are the detailed instructions described in Example 1.1, such as "cook" and "take." This library file (and there may be multiple library files opened) will contain all the additional source code necessary for the compiler to process your instructions. Thus, when you issue a simple command like "cook" you hope that someone else has written the detailed instructions explaining how to "cook" and that there is a library containing these instructions. In most programming languages, these types of instructions are called **keywords**.

Definition 1.3

Keywords are reserved instructions that are predefined actions in a programming language.

The Executable File

When the entire compilation process is complete, the object file and the needed pieces from the library file are merged together to create a machine language file called an **executable file**. For most compilers, this executable file contains all the needed instructions to run the program. This type of file most often has the extension **.exe** in Intel-based system and is a common sight on any computer. A true executable file is not readable by most individuals. The **.exe** file is stored in binary form and copies of the file may be distributed to anyone who needs to run it. The compiler itself is an example of an executable file as you are running a program when you use the compiler system. The most common end-user terminology for an executable file is an **application**.

Various C++ Compilers Currently Available

There are a great many C++ compilers available on the market today. As this is the most common application development language, many companies want to provide products to meet the needs of programmers. The trend is towards development kits or programming workbenches in which many useful tools are gathered to facilitate the rapid and easy development of programs. Available products range from freeware compilers that provide only a means to create executables to expensive work environments designed for commercial application development. The following list of some of the compilers and the operating systems for which they were designed is not exhaustive but constitutes an overview of the tools available today.

Compiler (alphabetical except freeware)	Operating Systems Supported
Borland C++ Development Tools	Windows
Borland Turbo C++ Visual Edition	Windows
CodeWarrior	MAC, UNIX, BeOs
DeltaPro C++	UNIX
IBM Visual Age C++	Windows, AIX, Solaris
Intel C/C++	Windows
Microsoft Visual C++	Windows
Microsoft Visual C++ .NET	Windows
NDP C/C++	OS/2
Symantec C++	Windows
Watcom C/C++	Windows, DOS, OS/2
Zortech C++	MAC, DOS

Compiler (alphabetical except freeware)	Operating Systems Supported
GNU Freeware	UNIX
DJGPP Freeware	UNIX

In addition, there are numerous compilers available for C++ that support mainframe operating systems, such as MVS, and mini-computer operating systems, such as OS/400. There are most certainly additional C++ compilers available, but those listed are some of the most common.

Microsoft Versions of Visual C++

As with any software, Microsoft supports and modifies its C++ compiler on a regular basis. In addition, Microsoft uses a segmentation strategy to appeal to different market segments with different versions of their C++ compiler. Currently, Microsoft is supporting four versions of .NET:

- Academic Edition
- Professional Edition
- Enterprise Developer Edition
- Enterprise Architect Edition

Microsoft Visual C++ is a development environment rather than simply a compiler. This environment includes an editor and many basic tools as well as Microsoft Foundation Classes to support the development of both traditional batch-oriented applications as well as WIN32 Applications.

Definition 1.4

Microsoft Foundation Classes provide prewritten tools in C++ to allow developers to quickly build new applications by utilizing program source code developed by others.

Definition 1.5

WIN32 Applications are programs that run in the Windows 95, Windows 98, Windows 2000, Windows XP, and Windows NT environments. These are applications such as MS-Word or other programs designed to run using Windows as a platform.

All four versions of .NET include the C++ compiler and basic tools, but the editions are designed for different types of users. The C++ engine with .NET provides everything from a basic platform for writing simple programs to an elaborate interface for combining C++ applications into XML Web development and distributed Web-based applications in C++. This creates a much more powerful C++ because applications written in this language can be distributed like Java or other Web-based languages.

Academic Edition

This package is targeted to academic users who are developing C++ (and .NET) courses. The edition includes tools and other components to facilitate team interaction and file sharing using the .NET environment in an academic setting. The product was specifically designed for use in the classroom.

Professional Edition

This is the standard package that includes the development environment and tools for average users wishing to pursue development in C++ using the power of .NET to build Web applications.

Enterprise Developer Edition

This version includes tools for sharing code (for Extreme Programming approaches) and team interaction in the workplace. It also provides life cycle management tools as a means to assist developers in the enterprise as they create new applications.

Enterprise Architect Edition

This edition takes the Enterprise Developer and adds tools for the development of systems in the enterprise. It specifically focuses on architecture and functionality as well as visual design of XML.

Support for Visual C++ on the Web

As with most texts today, we provide additional information and source code downloads for all the tutorials in this text. In addition, addenda and errata for this book may be found on the Web. We also provide a listing of common sources of help for Visual C++ and Visual Studio users on the Internet in this section.

Support for this text

doug.white@acm.org	The author's e-mail address
cislab.unco.edu/dwhite	Website for files and errata

Support for Visual C++

www.microsoft.com	Microsoft's Visual C++ site
www.functionx.com/visualc	A site supporting complex application development
www.tek-tips.com	A site with many forums including MSVC++
codeguru.earthweb.com	A C++ programming site

2 Creating Projects

I n Visual C++ .NET, programs are written as components of projects. In the past, many programs were written as simple stand-alone source code files (.cpp) without any means of encapsulating them into large scale projects. As you learn to program, you will find that programs today are not simply single source codes, but collections of files and libraries used to develop applications rapidly. In your first experiences with programming, you may indeed be working only with single source code files, but you will rapidly encounter the use of **header** files (**.h**) and other libraries as your programming skills develop.

A project allows all of the files being used to be gathered together in one project file. This facilitates the programming task, since the programmer may need to move between files as the application is developed. The project concept encourages good programming style by making it easier to create code in separate locations and avoid messy unmanaged code (often called spaghetti code).

This chapter provides you with information on the following topic:
- How to create a new project

Creating a New Project Tutorial

You should use projects to manage your files while you are working with Visual C++ .NET. This is the standard approach to designing programs in this environment. In this tutorial, we will create a new project and add some files to the project.

1. Start Visual C++.

Figure 2.1
The Start Page

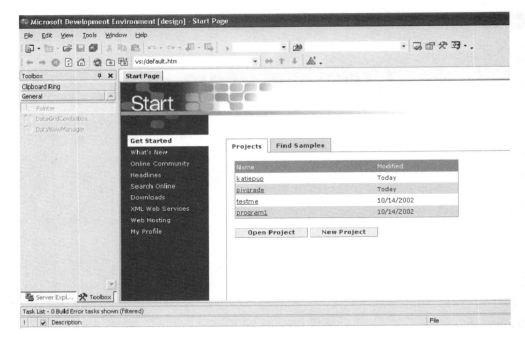

2. You should see the Start Page (see Figure 2.1). If you don't, you can always use the File menu to create new items.

3. Click on the **New Project** Box on the Start Page to generate a new project workspace (see Figure 2.2).

Figure 2.2
New Project Box

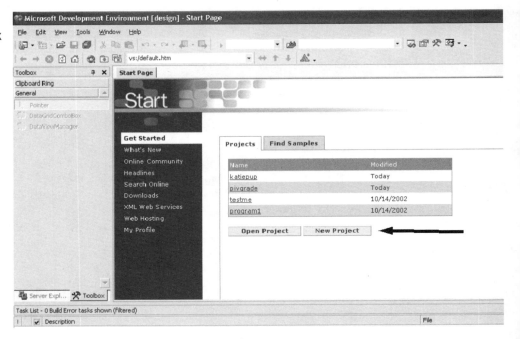

Figure 2.3
Win 32 Template
Project

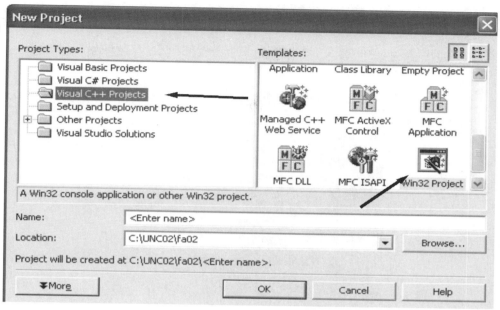

4. This will open the New Project wizard. Select a **Visual C++** project type and a **Win 32 Template** (see Figure 2.3).
5. Enter a name for the project and either enter a directory or use the Browse button to locate a directory to store the project. In this case, we will enter the filename myProj1 and the directory (which I have already created) called netFun (see Figure 2.4).

Figure 2.4
Enter a Filename

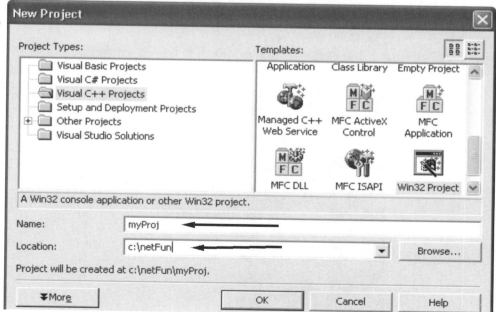

Figure 2.5
Application
Settings Tab

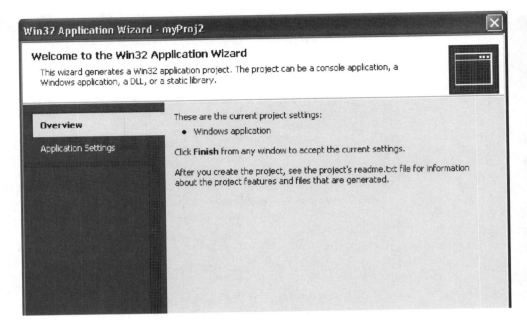

6. Click on the **OK** button.
7. The Win32 Application Wizard should start and you will need to specify some settings. Choose the Applications Settings Tab (see Figure 2.5).
8. This should take you to the options for the application (see Figure 2.6).

Figure 2.6
Application
Options

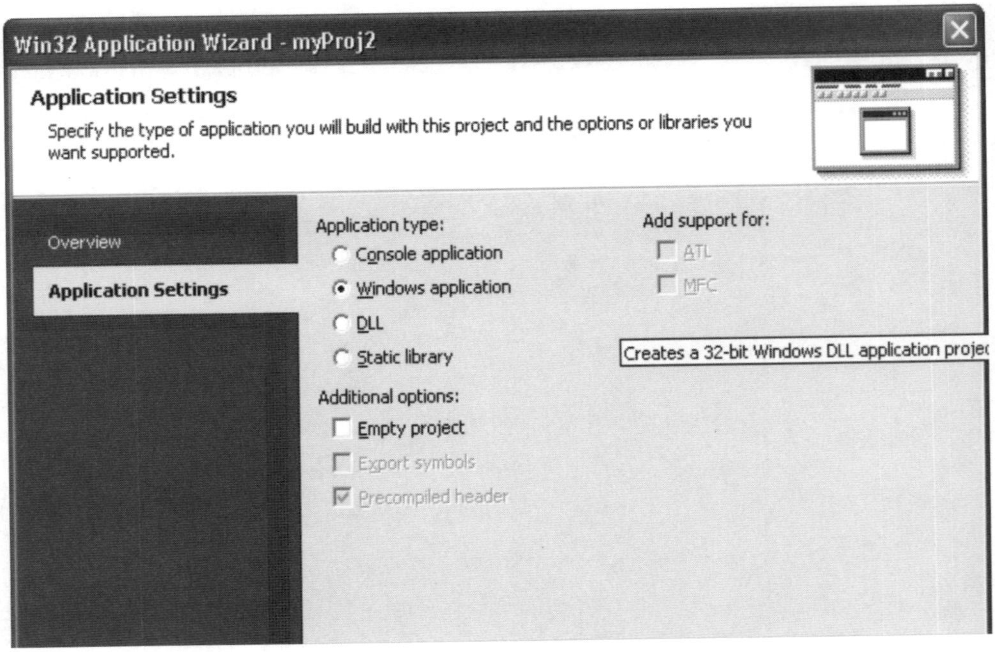

Figure 2.7
Console
Application

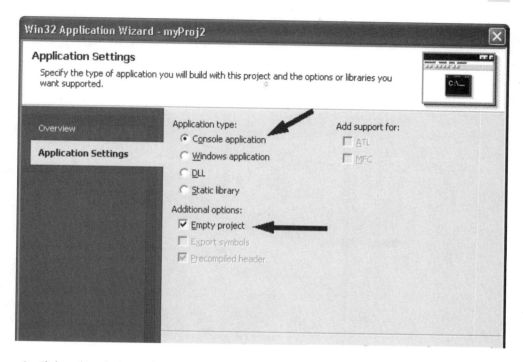

9. Click on the radio button for **Console application** and the check box for **Empty project** (see Figure 2.7).
10. Click the **Finish** button. You should then see the Start Page and the new project in the **Solution Explorer** window (see Figure 2.8).

Figure 2.8
Solution Explorer

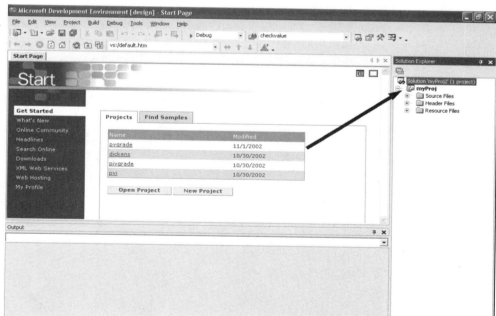

Figure 2.9
Save

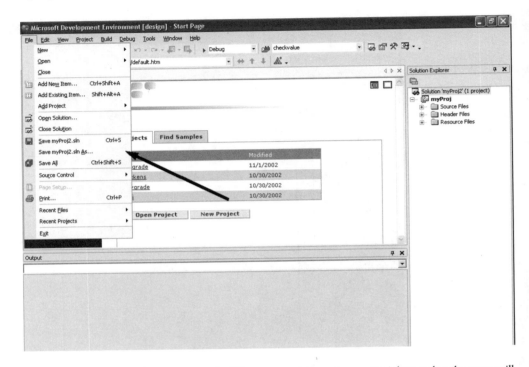

11. If you need to save the project, use the **File** menu and chose Save myProj (remember the name will reflect your project's name (see Figure 2.9).

At this point, you have created a new project and it is saved on your disk. You can add files, write source codes, create headers, and so forth inside the project. You should create new projects for each separate assignment or task.

3 Creating Source Code Files

Programmers spend most of their time working with source code files. It is a good idea to find a text editor that is both functional and comfortable for you to work with. For this reason, many programmers use the same editor (e.g., TECO, VI, or SOS) for many years on different mainframes although they were programming in different languages. Today, your first inclination may be to use a familiar word processing program to generate source code. This is not a good idea. Most compiler systems today function within an environment designed for development in a specific language. Visual C++ includes a development environment (and an editor) for the development of source codes in Visual C++.

There are any number of ways you can generate source code files, and any text editor (including TECO, VI, and SOS) will allow you to create C++ source code, but only an environment can provide all the tools to make this process efficient and easy, particularly for beginning programmers. This chapter provides you with information on the following topics:

- ASCII source files
- Developing source files using Visual C++ .NET
- Managing source files
- Managing header files
- Developing a source file in a practice exercise

ASCII Source Files

As mentioned earlier, ASCII is a basic symbol set that is used for Intel-based systems. C++, like most programming languages of the past (ASCII is a recent development), processes text files that can be generated using any application capable of creating them. One advantage of ASCII text files is that the files can be exchanged and read by almost any ASCII-based product.

There are no advanced formatting tools for dealing with ASCII files. This means you don't have to worry about underlines, fonts, or other formatting features. In fact, it's not possible to include formatting in an ASCII text file since only ASCII symbols are supported.

InfoBox

WINXX[1] supports filenames that are similar to LINUX/UNIX[2] type filenames. Very limited rules govern their use. Most file extensions are three spaces long based on the MS-DOS requirement of a filename that has no more than eight characters on the left of the dot (.) and three on the right. Common extensions are .exe, .txt, .doc, .cpp, and so forth.

Today, WINXX-based systems recognize files based on "associations" that use the MS-DOS type extensions to recognize file types. Thus, if you decide to use some unconventional system for your files on a WINXX system, you may find the system won't recognize them automatically. This may cause a great deal of difficulty for other users, and it may actually make locating your own files difficult later if you forget what sort of system you invented.

If you do decide to edit your C++ source files with something besides the Visual C++ environment editor, you should take care to save your files as ASCII, DOS Text, MS-DOS Text, Plain Text, or Text type files with the extension **.cpp**. Most editing software will attempt to put other extensions on the file, such as **.txt** or **.asc**, when you save it so you must specify **.cpp** as the type. Most C++ compilers will recognize any filename but non-standard file extensions create complications for beginning programmers.

The name on the left side of the dot (.) is more open to discussion. Many programmers come up with complex schema for naming files or follow what they were taught or what was required by their company. Some production environments (e.g., a commercial programming operation) may have a given schema for consistency among all programmers. The cwompany may use a different schema for test applications versus finalized production applications.

I suggest a standard approach for students: save source files using a significant portion of your last name and the assignment number. Thus, my files for programming assignments two and five (respectively) look like the following:

whitePII.cpp and **whitePV.cpp**

Some people have lengthy last names that, while they are supported, create unwieldy filenames. For those situations, I recommend eight letters and the program name. Yet, it's good to have a system that works for you. Your instructors may have some other schema that is more appropriate for you and the environment in which you work so please consult with them regarding filenames.

InfoBox

Mainframe and minicomputers do not follow these rules. Keep in mind that this text focuses on the use of Intel-based systems running WINXX. So, don't be surprised by filenames that defy all recognition if you are using VMS, MVS, OS/400, or other operating systems. Also, don't forget that the conventions used here are not rules, merely guidelines to help you.

---

[1] It is very common for programmers and other IT professionals to refer to operating systems that have multiple versions (e.g., Windows 98, Windows 95, Windows NT) by an abbreviation such as WINXX to imply any of those versions.

[2] Linux, by Linus Torvalds, and Unix (the basis for Linux) are extremely popular operating systems with network administrators, programmers, etc. Linux currently is the main competition against Microsoft's operating systems.

Common C++ Usages and Conventions

In C++, as in any language, there are rules, standards, and conventions that programmers need to understand if they are to use the language successfully. While it is not the purpose of this text to instruct you in the use of C++, some common features should be discussed with regard to development of source codes in C++.

Case Sensitivity in C++

C++ is a case-sensitive programming language. For many programmers, this is a difficult issue. In the past, programmers often used all uppercase or all lowercase letters for everything and never even thought about case. In C++, names and other terms are all subject to case. This means that a≠A and doug ≠ Doug in the eyes of C++ and the C++ compiler. Beginning programmers need to exhibit extra care in dealing with this issue, as many syntax errors will result purely due to the misuse of case in source code.

In ASCII, every symbol has a number that is unique to that symbol. A lowercase 'a' has the ASCII number (converted to decimal for convenience) 97, and a capital 'A' has the ASCII number 65. Since the computer uses binary numbers for everything, it cannot even consider that a == A since 97 ≠ 65 under any circumstances. It is critical that you adopt a convention for naming things in C++ that will allow you to remember how you deal with this issue. We will discuss some rules and some conventions that are used in C++ to help you get started.

Keywords

Every programming language has specific instructions called *keywords* that are standard in the language. If you recall Example 1.1, our robot knew how to "cook" and "take" things. In the same manner, C++ has many keywords that are defined for the compiler.

It is worth noting that when programmers define new keywords they can break all the rules and create keywords that don't follow any standard. Therefore, if in our example with the robot, we decide to create a new instruction that tells it how to "open" something, it is quite all right with the C++ compiler (since we wrote the instructions ourselves) but it may confuse others and you later since open ≠ Open to the compiler.

Comments in Programming

Most programming languages encourage the creation of commentary in the body of the source code. The programmer may insert comments about what is happening, why it is happening, and other issues for all to see. This greatly assists in the reading and analysis of the program.

RealWorld

In the real world, organizations often have specific commenting requirements that programmers must use for consistency. Comments may link the lines of code to informational tools or plans, such as flowcharts, data flow diagrams, and pseudocodes. Many comments in your programs will be helpful to your systems analyst and make your code easier to integrate with others'. Although there are certainly real-world programmers I have worked with who use little or no commentary in their programs, unless you are a solo coder, you will find a real need for comments, even if comments are not a requirement.

Real-world programmers often work on many projects simultaneously and may have to switch from one project to another. Sometimes, programmers must return to work supposedly completed months or even years earlier. You will find that in this environment you need to be able to get into the code quickly and cannot spend days trying to remember what you were doing and why you were doing it. Commentary is often your only guide.

Properly designated commentary is ignored by the compiler and allows the programmer to write comments in plain English (or any other language/structure he or she wishes). This is a very useful tool for making source code readable. When a comment symbol is detected by the compiler, the compiler ignores the commentary and no errors are generated.

Figure 3.1
In-line
Comments

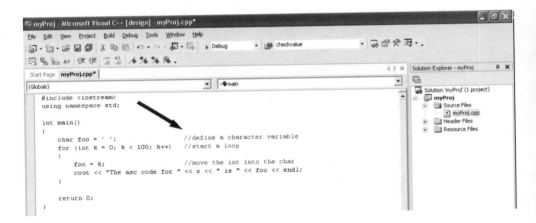

C++ provides for commentary in the form of both **in-line comments** and **block comments**. In addition, **document comments** (usually just called doc comments) are also available.

Definition 3.1

In-line comments are included on a line of source code. These comments are usually used to describe in English what a specific instruction in C++ is intended to do.

Definition 3.2

Block comments are long sections of commentary that often appear at the beginning and in other key locations of the source code. This type of commentary usually provides documentation of various structures, explanations of what is supposed to happen, information on how to utilize the source code in different situations, references to flowcharts or other planning materials, and/or general information about the program.

Figure 3.2
Block
Comments

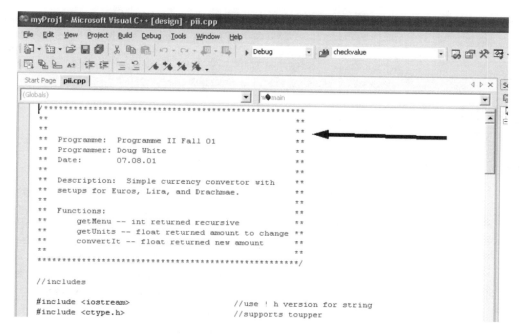

Definition 3.3

....

Doc comments are designed to be extracted by other programs to use in the creation of documentation for code to be published separately. Visual C++ supports this feature and it is expected that this type of commentary will gain in popularity as more source codes are shared and reused within companies and across the Internet. Doc comments allow the generation of a file of documentation in a consistent manner.

In Visual C++, in-line comments are created by using the // symbol. This informs the compiler to ignore the rest of the physical line. The symbol /* is used together with */ to create a block comment in which everything contained within the block is ignored.

Scope Delimiters

Most programming languages have **scope delimiters**.

Definition 3.4

....

A *scope delimiter* is a symbol or pair of symbols used to define a region or area that is considered a locale. For instance, in the United States, many states used rivers or other natural features as boundaries for their scope. In programming, many structures need to have their scope defined because they should not affect the entire program. Thus, symbols are used to define scopes in pairs.

In C++, the symbols { and } are used as scope delimiters. These rarely used symbols became popular with the advent of C, which used them as well. It is important that you understand there is a difference between { } (curly braces or braces), ( ) (parentheses), and [ ] (square brackets or brackets). They are not equivalent and have different ASCII numbers. Your text will include detailed descriptions of where and how these delimiters are used in C++ programs.

Literals

Most programming languages allow programmers to use **literals**.

Definition 3.5

Literals are system commands or other pieces of information that the compiler doesn't understand. Compilers are written to serve as general-purpose tools and often run on many different operating systems. This means that if the programmer has some specific instruction for the user or the operating system, he or she may have to use the operating system's rule set (syntax) instead. As the compiler can't possibly know all rule sets, these items are classified as literals by the compiler and special instructions are used to manage them, as seen in Example 3.1.

Example 3.1

Revisit our robot and consider the following instruction:
Say hello to our guest in Mandarin Chinese
你好
Now, as you might guess, the robot has no idea what these symbols mean, but an instruction such as
Display "你好" to our guest
may be carried out even if the robot has no idea why or what it is saying.

In C++, literals are enclosed in " " (quotes). The symbols tell the compiler that this is something to be used with the operating system or the user, and a different set of rules applies. The most common use of this type of literal is to manage files in an operating system. While Visual C++ was designed to run in WINXX, many other operating systems are supported as well. If the programmer needs a file in VAX/VMS or MVS, the instructions for getting it may differ wildly from the commands used in WINXX.

In C++ and other ASCII-based editors there is no end quote, so the quotes used for both beginning and ending are the same straight quote. In modern word processing, however, reverse quotes are often used. There is no ASCII number for the reverse quote symbol, but it is not used in C++ programming. Always use the keyboard " (shift + apostrophe) for all quote usage in C++ source code.

Columns and White Space in C++

For many years programming was very structured, as it had evolved from the use of punched cards, which were based on columns. The COBOL, FORTRAN, and RPG programming languages all used punched cards in the 60s and 70s as a means of generating lines of source code (one line per card) and the cards were all based on everything being in certain columns. Some languages, such as RPG III, were extremely column oriented and required great care in the development of source code.

As you may guess, this was very tedious for programmers since they had to manage the columns and be very accurate with their placement of instructions or they would have many complaints from the compiler. Modern programming languages, for the most part, have gone to "free-form" approaches that use **delimiters** instead of columns to determine the end of instructions.

Definition 3.6

A *delimiter* is a symbol that terminates an instruction or set of instructions. In the English language, a period (.) is used as a delimiter so that readers of English can still make sense of

"A   lot   of
spacing   and line   feeds   are used
here   to   make   a
point."

In C++, the delimiter used is a semi-colon (;). C++ doesn't care about columns and the amount of white space used in a line of C++ source code. There are certainly conventions that we will discuss for formatting C++ source code, but as far the compiler is concerned, all of the source code could appear on one gigantic line. This would certainly make the programmers job of editing difficult and would likely result in violence on the part of a system's analyst or instructor, though the compiler would be perfectly happy.

Most modern programmers tend to use indents (tabs), blank lines, and other strategies to make their programs more readable. There are "spaghetti coders" who write confused, complicated programs that nevertheless work, but you should not follow their examples.

Indentation Conventions and Subordination

With the advent of free-form programming came the advent of indentation in source code. Most real-world programmers work in teams or must submit portions of their code for approval from time to time. (This of course excludes gonzo, underground, game programmers who live in someone's basement, eat nothing but refried beans and Cheetos, and hope for a break into the big time someday.) Thus, programmers attempt to make their code easily legible by using white space and tabs.

Many programming instructions become subordinate to other instructions due to scope or other restrictions. Formatting the code to reflect this subordination helps the reader of the code understand its inherent logic.

Example 3.2

Let's assume we have another command for our robot. This command says "if," allowing the robot to make a clear choice based on some criteria. So, we can say:

If the user chooses Chinese as a language, then display "你好"

Otherwise, display "Hello"

In Example 3.2, the display command is subordinate to the condition required to obtain that display, so we might write the instructions using tabs (indents) to indicate clearly these conditional responses. For example:

If Chinese
   Display "你好"
Otherwise
   Display "Hello"

This type of indentation allows the programmer (and others) to spot subordination in the program quickly and may help later in the understanding of problems that emerge due to misuse of subordination. It is worth noting that C++ does not care about this use of white space and would be satisfied with:

If Chinese Display "你好"Otherwise Display "Hello"

Example 3.3

The following segment of C++ source code illustrates the use of comments, indentations, and white space.

```cpp
#include <iostream>
using namespace std;

/********************************************************
**                                                    **
**                                                    **
**     Program:     ASCII Display program             **
**     Programmer:  Doug White                        **
**                                                    **
**     Simple program to display all the decimal codes for all  **
**     of the ASCII and extended ASCII char sets.  The program  **
**     runs through all the numbers in a loop and prints the    **
**                                                    **
**     number and the ASCII character on the screen.  **
**                                                    **
**                                                    **
********************************************************/

void main()
{
    char foo;                              //Define a Character variable
                                           //        named foo
    for (int x = 0; x<10000; x++)    //Start a Loop
    {
        foo = x;                           //assign the value of x to foo

        cout << "asc" << x << " is " << foo << endl;
    }
}
```

Case Conventions in C++

The most common practice among C++ programmers is to use small letters for the first part of a variable name and a capital letter to begin the second part.

Example 3.4

*If you create a name in C++ (called a **variable** or **identifier**) that will be used to hold some information about weight, you might name that variable theWeight using this popular naming convention.*

This convention is widely followed for most names the programmer creates in his or her source code. This helps programmers avoid using keywords (remember they are all lowercase) as names. The same convention is also used in the Java, Visual Basic, and C programming languages and has become a standard convention in programming.

RealWorld

Remember that programmers often do unusual things and fail to follow convention. Companies also make their own conventions for their own reasons, and you may encounter many programs in the real world that have totally different standards.

Hungarian Notation

Hungarian notation is an approach to defining names in programming in which a descriptive prefix is attached to any given variable name. As this is a convention, there are many variants and many programmers ignore it completely. Essentially, Hungarian notation involves the attempt to identify a variable by its type and use in the program. For instance, a signed integer variable might be named iMyInt in C++ using Hungarian notation. A float might be described as fMyFloat. Your instructor may or may not wish to discuss this type of notation in your course.

Color Coding in Visual C++

If you use the Visual C++ editor to develop your source codes, you will find that the editor does everything it can to assist you in the development of error-free code. One way it does this is through automatic color coding for all the ANSI standard components of C++.

Comments

All comments (both block and in-line) in C++ will appear color coded in green to indicate that these instructions are considered commentary and are being ignored by the compiler. In Figure 3.3, we see both types of comments displayed on the screen by the C++ editor. (**NOTE**: The text in this book does not appear in color, but these comments in the Visual Studio development environment will appear in green as indicated.)

In Figure 3.3, notice that the programmer has used block comments (starting with /*) at the top of the program to describe the program and then used in-line comments throughout this listing to identify various structures in the C++ program. If you are using a computer, notice that on the in-line comments, only the comment (the part ignored by the C++ processor) is shown in green.

Figure 3.3
Two Sets of
Comments

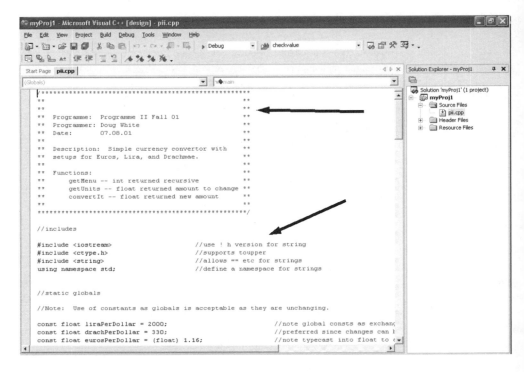

NOTE: It is possible to accidentally create comments where they were unexpected. In Figure 3.4, a programmer has forgotten to terminate his block commentary with */ and now he essentially has no source code as it is all ignored by the compiler.

Figure 3.4
Comment Errors

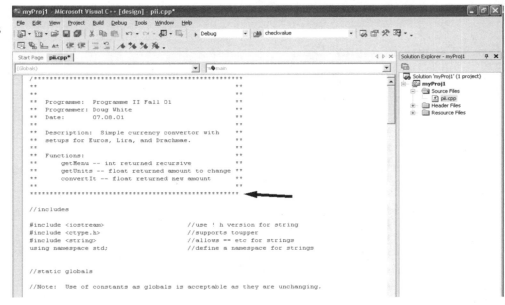

The programmer should always take note of green comment code and make sure that comments are only where he or she expected them and are not affecting the rest of the source code in any way. There is more discussion on this topic in the section on debugging.

Keywords

All ANSI keywords in C++ are coded in blue. You can use this feature to spot the proper and improper use of keywords. For instance, when examining the screen shown in Figure 3.5, you notice that the keyword is blue in two instances and black in another (indicated by the arrow). See if you can spot the reason for the difference.

Figure 3.5
Keywords

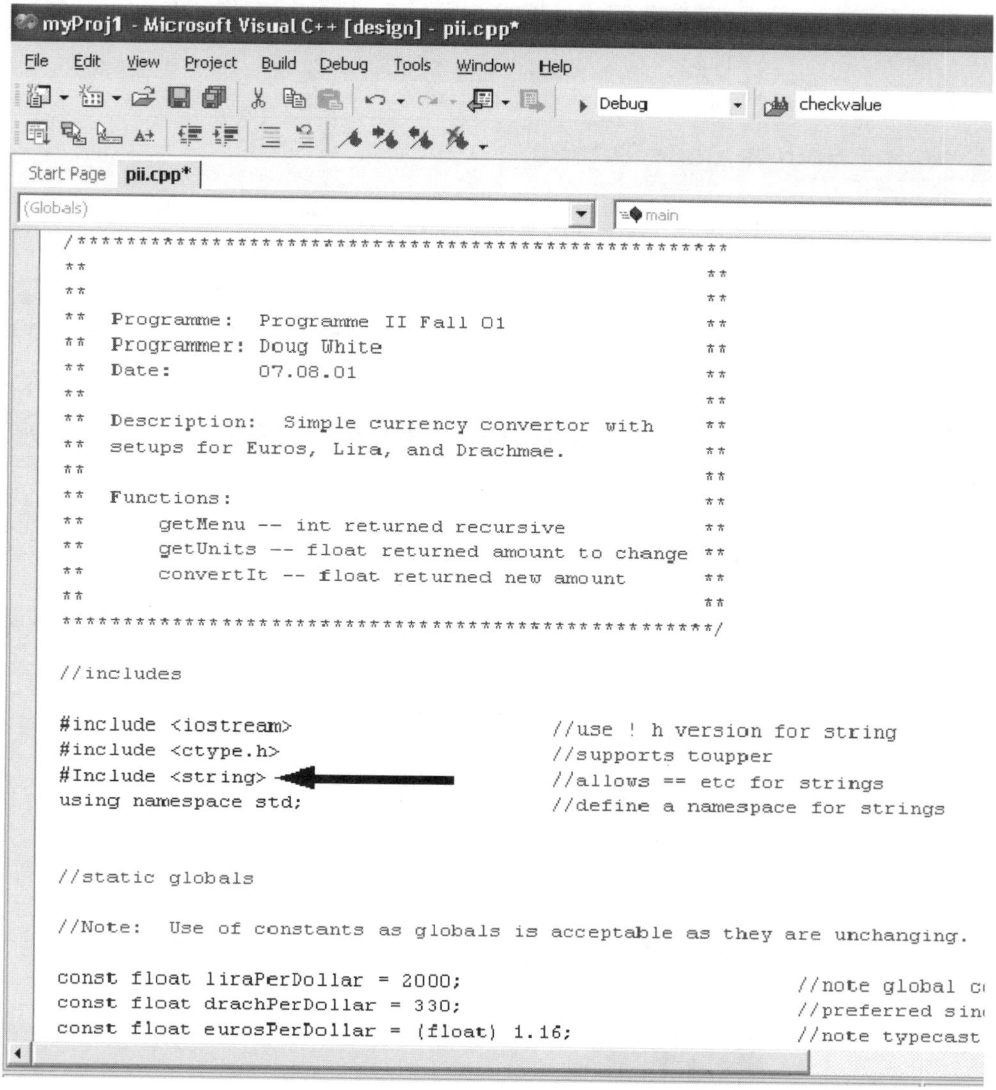

```
/ ***********************************************************
**                                                        **
**                                                        **
**   Programme:  Programme II Fall 01                     **
**   Programmer: Doug White                               **
**   Date:        07.08.01                                **
**                                                        **
**   Description:  Simple currency convertor with         **
**   setups for Euros, Lira, and Drachmae.                **
**                                                        **
**   Functions:                                           **
**       getMenu -- int returned recursive                **
**       getUnits -- float returned amount to change      **
**       convertIt -- float returned new amount           **
**                                                        **
************************************************************/

//includes

#include <iostream>              //use ! h version for string
#include <ctype.h>               //supports toupper
#Include <string>  <----         //allows == etc for strings
using namespace std;             //define a namespace for strings


//static globals

//Note:  Use of constants as globals is acceptable as they are unchanging.

const float liraPerDollar = 2000;         //note global c
const float drachPerDollar = 330;         //preferred sin
const float eurosPerDollar = (float) 1.16;  //note typecast
```

The difference is that the second indicated keyword **#Include** is capitalized by mistake. This causes the compiler to fail to recognize #Include as an ANSI keyword. Remember that Include ≠ include and that all the ANSI keywords in C++ are lowercase. After you use the editor for a bit, you will quickly take note when you type in a keyword and it doesn't turn blue. The bad news is that after you get used to this system, it is hard to use a non-environment type editor because you are constantly wondering why the color didn't change.

Non-ANSI Keywords

One point to note about C++ is that there are many additional non-ANSI keywords that are in frequent use. The compiler has no idea what these keywords are, so they do not appear in blue. Just like names you create, names created by other programmers and used by you are considered "other" by the compiler and will always appear in plain black type. Two very common keywords are **cin** and **cout**. These non-ANSI keywords are added by programmers when they want to do input and output to the screen. Unless at some future date they are added to the ANSI standard, they will always appear in black typeface because the compiler doesn't recognize them as standard keywords.

Creating Source Code Tutorial

You now have enough information to type in a source code file. At this point, we want to walk through creating a new file of source code and then typing a simple program into the editor. We won't run the program in this tutorial.

You should start .NET either by clicking on the icon or using the Start menu. If you did the tutorial in Chapter 2 to create the myProj project, you should see the screen shown in Figure 3.6. Notice myProj is listed. (If you didn't do the tutorial, do it now or create a project for use here.)

Figure 3.6
Visual C++ Start
Up (with an
empty project)

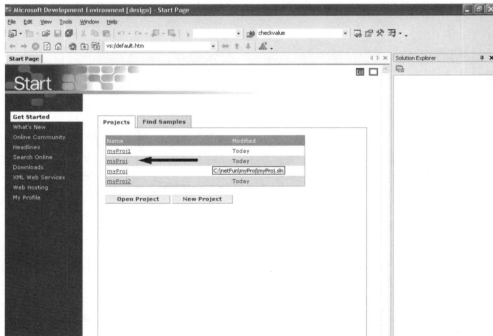

This is an empty project, and you should verify that you are indeed in Visual C++ by looking in the upper-left corner of the program.

Figure 3.7
The Visual C++
Verify

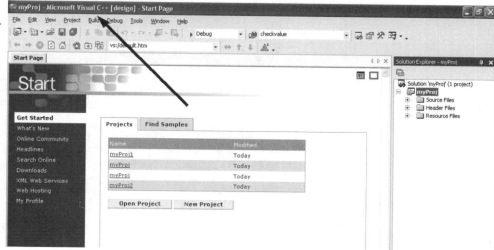

The only reason to do this is because you may have run the wrong application when choosing from the menu—several other applications look very similar to Visual C++ (Visual Basic is one).

  .NET defaults to the last project you worked on, so the myProj project may already be open if you just did the Chapter 2 tutorial. Look in the upper-left corner at the **Solution Explorer** to see if myProj is the current project. If myProj is not open, click on the recent projects item in the Start page (see Figure 3.8) or choose Open Solution from the File menu (see Figure 3.9).

Figure 3.8
Start Page

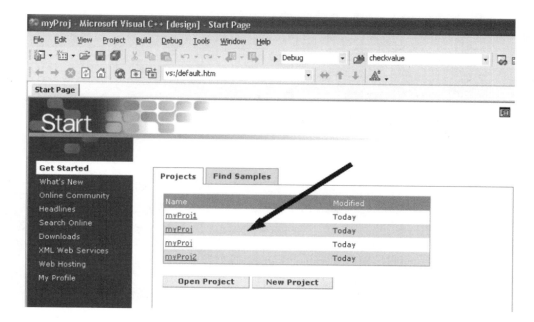

Figure 3.9
File Menu

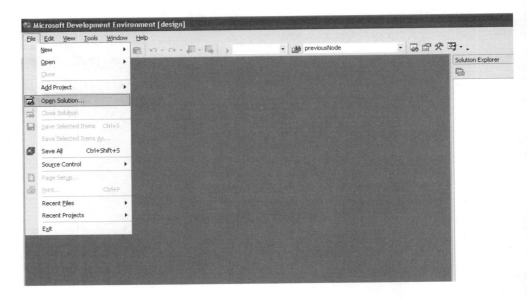

At this point, the screen should have myProj in the Solution Explorer window. You should now add an empty C++ source file (**.cpp**) to the project. The simplest way to do this is by right-clicking on the folder in the Solution Explorer window called **Source Files** (see Figure 3.10). Choose **Add** and then **Add New Item** from the menu to create a new **.cpp file**.

Figure 3.10
Source Files

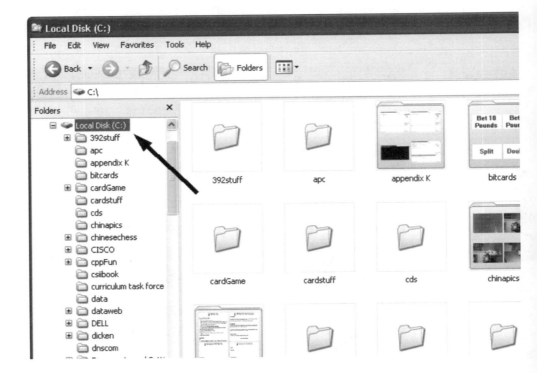

You will then see the **Add New Item** window displayed (see Figure 3.11). This is where you name and locate the new file. You can save the file in a different directory from the project, but for general use, it is a good idea to put the file with the project. I named the file myFirstCpp. Click on the **C++ File icon** and then type myFirstCpp in the **Name** box. The project directory is below the **Name** box (see Figure 3.12). If you want to change the location of the file, you can do that in the **Location** box.

Figure 3.11
Add New Item

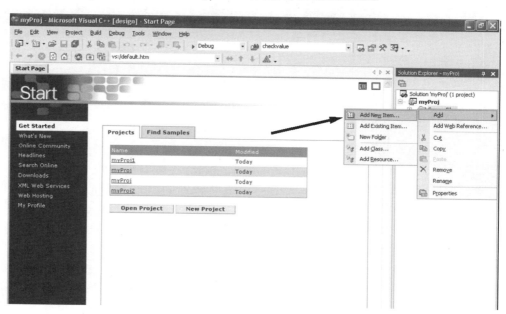

Figure 3.12
Name Box

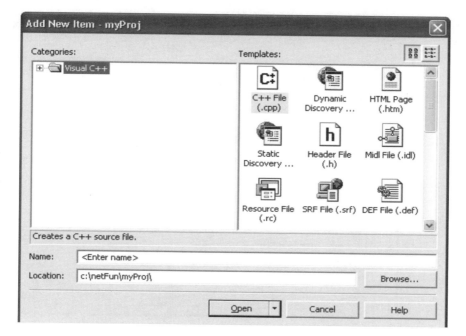

Now, click on the **Open** button to get into the new, blank file (see Figure 3.13). You should then see the workspace for the source code (see Figure 3.14). Notice that in the Solution Explorer and in the upper-left corner, the filename is indicated to help you remember where you are working. This is particularly useful if you have multiple files open at any given time.

Figure 3.13
Open Button

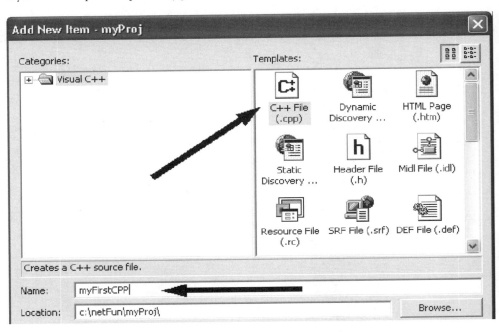

Figure 3.14
Workspace

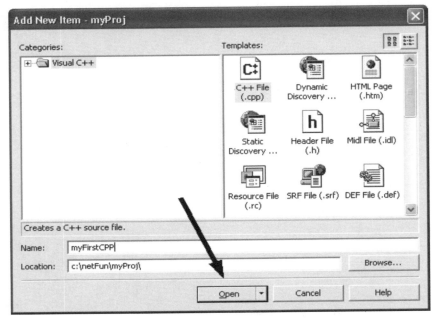

You can begin typing in source code and commentary in the edit window and continue until you are finished. I suggest you save your work often since there is no autosave in Visual C++. If there is a power failure or other problem, you may lose all the typing you have done.

One interesting feature of the Visual C++ editor is the intelligent indentation and pair matching of scope delimiters. The editor will attempt to line up all the code if you let it. So, when you are typing the sample program into the editor, take note of how the editor indents the code since it usually knows what it is doing. With minor exceptions, the layout of the lines and white space will not matter but try to reproduce the following program.

In the following example, you should type *exactly* the source code that is given, paying particular attention to the case of the example. Your instructor may wish to give you a different sample program to enter here, but you can always use this one for practice. It is a very simple program thatdoesn't make use of the structured approach to programming (the use of functions), so it would be called "spaghetti code" by most programmers. However, the program should prove to be simple to type and a good exercise for beginning programmers in getting the code in place.

Example 3.5

Source Listing for Birthstone Program

```
/*********************************************************************
**    Program:     Example Exercise 3.5 from Visual C++ Text    **
**    Programmer:  Doug White                                   **
**    Date:        June 27, 2002                                **
**                                                              **
**    This is a very simple program to provide a first program **
**    experience for beginning programmers in Visual C++ 6.0.  **
**    The program asks the user for their birthday month and then**
**    determines their birthstone based the month they were    **
**    born.                                                     **
**                                                              **
*********************************************************************/
#include <iostream>                              //standard io file
#include <ctype.h>
using namespace std;

int main()
{
    //Main program

    int aMonth = 0;
    bool anAlien = false;
    char resp =  N ;

    do {
        cout <<  What numerical month were you born (1-12)?  << endl;
        cin >> aMonth;
        switch (aMonth)                          //test the data
        {
```

```
case 1:
{
    cout <<  Garnet   ;
    break;
}
case 2:
{
    cout <<  Amethyst   ;
    break;
}
case 3:
{
    cout <<  Aquamarine   ;
    break;
}
case 4:
{
    cout <<  Diamond   ;
    break;
}
case 5:
{
    cout <<  Emerald   ;
    break;
}
case 6:
{
    cout <<  Pearl   ;
    break;
}
case 7:
{
    cout <<  Ruby   ;
    break;
}
case 8:
{
    cout <<  Sardonyx   ;
    break;
}
case 9:
{
    cout <<  Sapphire   ;
    break;
}
case 10:
{
    cout <<  Opal   ;
    break;
}
```

```
            case 11:
            {
                cout <<   Topaz   ;
                break;
            }
            case 12:
            {
                cout <<   Turquoise   ;
                break;
            }
            default:
            {
                //something is wrong
                cout <<   Sorry, aliens are not covered ;
                cout <<   under this policy. Earth months only!  << endl;
                    anAlien = true;
                    break;
            }
        } //end switch

        if (!anAlien)
        {
            cout <<   is your birthstone!  << endl;
        }
        cout <<   Do another? (Y/N)  << endl;
        cin >> resp;
    }while (toupper(resp) ==  Y );
}
//the end
```

When you have finished with the source code, you should save your file by choosing the **File** menu then **Save** myProj.cpp (see Figure 3.15).

Figure 3.15
The File Save
Function

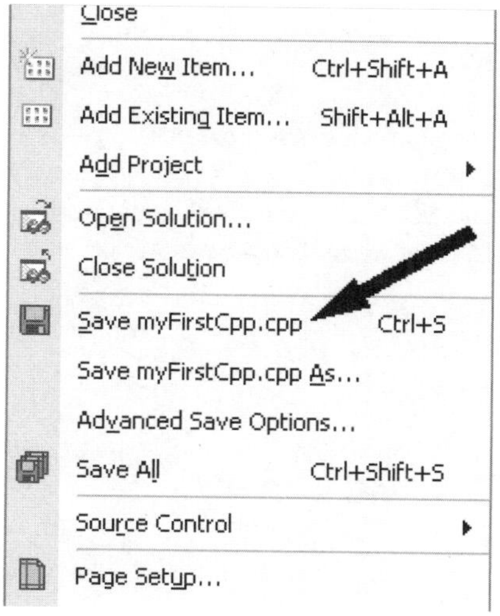

This completes the exercise for inputting source code. Go back and take careful note of the keywords, the commentary, and the white space in the program for future reference.

Running this Program (Optional)

You may want to run the program you have just entered. You should be prepared for it to contain errors, which may seem discouraging at this point. A suggestion is that you wait until you have finished the debugging tutorials in Chapter 4. However, if you really want to run the source code, just add the following steps to the tutorial (or use the Chapter 4 tutorial for more detail).

1.   Press the **Build Solution** button on the **Build menu** (see Figure 3.16) or just press F7.

Figure 3.16
The Build
Solution Menu

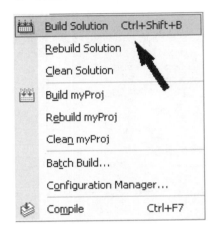

If the program compiles successfully (no errors), you will see what is shown in Figure 3.17.

2.   Then choose **Start without Debugging** from the **Debug** menu (see Figure 3.18) or press CTRL-F5.
     Again, if the program contains errors, wait until you have completed the debugging tutorials and come back and get some debugging practice. If there are no errors, then the program will run at this point and you can play with it.

Saving and Managing Source Code Files

In an educational setting as well as in the real world, it may prove necessary to develop a method for managing files to keep up with all the programs you write. Companies usually have a method for management of files and for their protection. This section discusses both protecting your work and managing files; as well as some useful approaches to development that are used in the real world.

Figure 3.17
The Successful
Compile

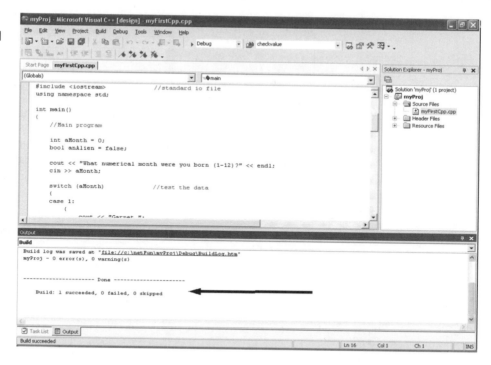

Figure 3.18
The Start without
Debugging Menu

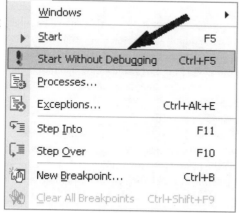

File Naming and Version Management

Everyone comes up with schema for naming things. Often these schemas are not very useful and end up adding to the confusion when you forget the clever approach you designed years ago. For instance, in my archive I have the file 101197phil.cob. It's a COBOL file and the numbers probably indicate a date. Phil is a former boss, so perhaps the file has something to do with him. Beyond that, there are no clues to its purpose.

As you start developing your own programs, you will encounter the need to maintain both backup copies and older versions of the code. Sometimes programmers, especially beginning programmers, make changes that are not necessarily the best. Their code gets so convoluted that they cannot sort it out and need to return to a previous version. I suggest you use the method common in the industry, version numbering. Admittedly, this means you have multiple copies of the program on your disk, but since most educational software is not that large, and in industry you should have plenty of storage space available, it's a good approach.

Software developers use a numbering system that has multiple parts to attempt to describe the changes that have taken place between versions. The numbers commonly look like 6.7.8.9. For our purposes, let's propose you maintain three files. Call them A, B, and C. In the industry, the first number from the left is used to describe the main version number and changes here represent total revisions of the program. A change to the A number may create a problem with backwards compatibility because a major change has taken place.

Definition 3.7

Backwards compatibility refers to the ability of a new version of an application to work with an older version. An example would be Visual C++ 6.0 being able to process files created with Visual C++ 5.0. (**NOTE**: As a rule, there is no "forwards compatibility.")

Each number you move to the right represents change at a lower and lower level of the code; for example, a change from 6.7.8.9 to 6.7.8.10 might represent only a minor modification affecting a tiny number of users.

Students should keep the three copies and use them as a version development approach. Assign the working file a name such as PIIIfa02.cpp for assignment 3 in Fall of 2002. When a milestone is accomplished that is worth saving (for example, the first draft of the source code), save an extra copy as PIIIAsp02.cpp in the same directory. You could return to this milestone if large-scale problems result when working on the source code later. The next time a milestone is accomplished, save the file as PIIIBfa02.cpp. Now, you have two copies of the program from different points in time. If the programmer really needed to, he or she could go back to A and start over from that point without too much trouble. PIIICfa02.cpp represents the next milestone. Usually programmers keep using the letters of the alphabet, and in academic development, you won't run out of letters. After a while, if you are having space limitation problems, you may want to delete some early versions of the code.

You can certainly extend the naming conventions in more complex projects to names such as A1 or B27 to distinguish minor milestones as well as major ones. This can save you a lot of work if you really get things muddled at three o'clock in the morning in the computer lab, not to mention the comfort of being able to return to a previous milestone instead of starting all over if you lose a file. Your instructor likely has some horror stories of lost files and late-night errors to share and may wish you to use his or her preferred approaches to file naming.

Disk Space Issues

Obviously, the best solution to disk space problems is to run Visual C++ on a hard disk drive that is large and almost empty. This option is not available to most people, but it is certainly the best solution. You are left primarily with a number of storage choices:

- Hard Disk Drive
- Floppy Disk Drive

- Zip Disk
- CD-R(W) Drive

You will find that source code and text files in general are quite small, usually insignificant in terms of the gigantic hard drives and other storage media available today. Even a 1 Megabyte floppy disk drive is large by text file standards.

The only real issue you will face is the storage of the secondary files for all the programs as they are created by Visual C++. Visual C++ creates six files for each program and some of these files can be two or three times the size of the source code file. Students usually run out of space on a floppy disk drive quite rapidly. Therefore, consider using a Zip disk or a different floppy disk for each project. As CD-R(W) drives become more commonplace, they offer another option for storage.

The only downside to having all your projects on your hard disk at home is that you may find you need to have the disk available at school. Imagine the following scenario: You drop by your instructor's office to report, "I think I am done," and she says, "How did you deal with the array?" You think, "What array? There was an array needed!" You would find it convenient to have your materials with you so you can modify your array.

In addition, you can delete any of the files except the source code files (**.cpp**) in your directory because they are all created by the compiler and can be recreated any time you wish simply by recompiling. The compiler will also create a "debug" folder that contains additional files and the **.exe** file for your program. These too can be deleted and recreated as needed.

Finally, remember that you will have problems with Visual C++ if you are out of disk space or even low on disk space (say 95% of the disk is full). This may cause your program to fail to run, Visual C++ to crash, or frustrating errors to occur during the compile process. Thus, you should always be aware of the amount of disk space available to you, especially if you are in a lab. I have heard tales of people being unable to save their work and losing it due to lack of disk space in a lab. If you want to check the disk space on a WinXX machine do the following:

1. Press the **Windows** and e keys simultaneously. You should see something similar to Figure 3.19.
2. Next, left-click on the device you want to check. Its capacity and free space will appear at the bottom of the window, as shown in Figure 3.20. You may also right-click the device and choose **Properties** for a more in-depth examination of the device.

As you can see in Figure 3.20 this is an 11.25 Gigabyte drive with 8.35 Gigabytes free. The user wouldn't have to worry. The project tutorial you completed earlier shows how much space a simple project in Visual C++ might take up. If you open the **netFun** directory, you should be able to see the size of the file you typed and the project containing it. Later, when we compile the files, you can check the size of the entire directory to get some idea of how much space you will need.

Backup Copies

It is vital that you make backup copies of your work. All storage media are subject to failures and the failures usually occur at inopportune moments such as the day an assignment is due.

Hard disks and even CDs are not immune to failure. You should always make backup copies, even though it will cost additional time before you can go home. Don't be the student who shows his or her instructor a 3.5-inch floppy disk that looks like a fried egg and asks, "It got really hot in my car and all my term projects are on this disk. Do you think you can get them back?" The answer is "No."

If you are storing the files on a floppy disk, then duplicate the disk on another floppy and make a copy on the hard drive of the machine if it's your machine. This makes several copies on different media. The same goes for a Zip disk or a CD. Make sure you have at least one extra copy of the file on a different media.

Figure 3.19
The Explorer
Screen

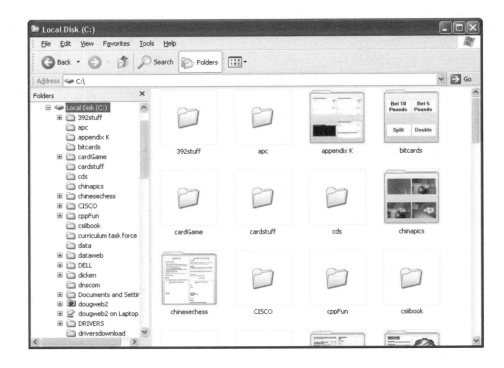

Figure 3.20
The Disk Space
Available

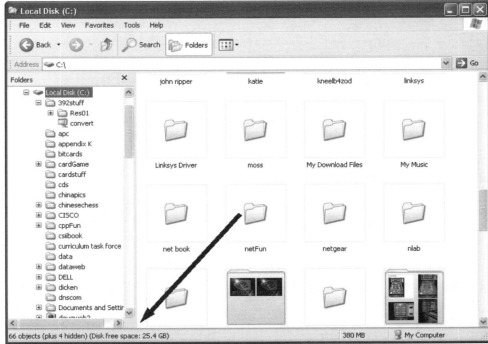

Name the files something with the extension .bak so you remember that they are backup files. If you need to restore them later, you can rename them.

One very important point to remember about backing up files on hard disks is that many labs and home computers are set up with **partitions** on the **physical drive** to create multiple logical drives.

Definition 3.8

A *partition* is a means of creating a barrier on a storage device such that separate drive letters may be assigned to each partition (e.g., C:, D:, E:).

Definition 3.9

A *physical drive* is a single drive unit such as a hard disk, a CD, or a floppy drive.

Definition 3.10

A *logical drive* is a drive that is contained in a physical device. Thus, many logical drives may share a single physical drive.

The danger is that if the physical drive fails, all of the logical drives on that device may also fail. Therefore, you should try to keep your source code files on separate media.

In addition, you need to protect the backup copies. If a backup copy is left in a drive, it might be stolen along with the computer. Identify a safe place and keep your backup copies all together there. In commercial applications, you might consider off-site storage, but in academic work, simply making a separate copy on a different media is sufficient.

Laboratory Storage and Other Security Issues for Programming Students

Computer labs are notorious locations for security problems. Everyone from expert hackers to novice programmers uses the facility, often at the same time. Several categories of problems manifest themselves when you are using any machine that is available to the public:

- Viruses
- Plagiarism
- Theft
- Malicious Mischief

Viruses

Computer viruses are virtually uncountable. If you look at some of the commercial anti-virus products, you will see literally hundreds of thousands of known virus definitions, let alone all the yet undiscovered viruses running around. It is the work of seconds to install a virus (often unwittingly) on a machine. Lab machines are notorious for having viruses since so many different people are using them and running software and disks through them. Likewise, e-mail-based viruses are constantly being passed around the Internet and sent to unsuspecting victims, often by other victims of the virus.

If you are transporting disks between home and school or receiving e-mail, you should have anti-virus software in place. Scan any disks you are taking home before you leave the lab. This will help ensure that you spread no viruses. You should also have anti-virus software in place on your home machine (or anywhere else you use these disks). Not all viruses are known and the anti-virus software in your lab may be dated or not working properly.

If you are e-mailing files back and forth or sharing them via the Web, the cautions also apply. Many viruses can be transported via e-mail or attached to files and Web pages. In addition, you need to make sure the anti-virus software you are using contains the most current virus definitions. Many people install the software and then never update it. Whatever software you are using should have a Website that will have updates for the file and instructions on how to use them. Commercial providers of anti-virus software are Mcaffee (www.mcaffee.com), Norton (www.norton.com), Symantec (www.symantec.com), and Computer Associates (www.ca.com). If you don't have anti-virus protection, you will have problems eventually.

Plagiarism

A second issue is plagiarism. Sadly, many people are too lazy to do their own work. Cheating happens. You need to protect your work, as there are sure to be some people who would rather steal your programs than learn how to make their own. If they are caught, they may not admit to the act but instead turn and accuse you. People get copies of others' work in several key ways:

- Shoulder Surfing
- Temp Directories
- Shared Directories
- Discarded Print
- New Print

Shoulder surfing is as old as Programming 101 and involves people wandering around the lab looking for "help" on their programs.

Temp directories are often placed on lab machines so that students can store their work temporarily. Most students neglect to delete their files from these directories when they finish working. Lab administrators or an automated process will eventually delete the files, but sometimes these directories are shared over a network! Cheaters will often cruise machines not in use, surfing for files such as CS1610PIII.cpp (or whatever) so they can acquire files to use or sell to others. If you are using temp directories on a lab machine, be sure to use generic names (like oldwork.tmp) and delete your files when you are done. This action will prevent others from finding your programs and copying them. You might even password protect or encrypt the files.

Sometimes, the temp or other directories used for public storage are shared across the lab. This is an open invitation for someone either to copy your files or just watch you do the work and then copy your changes. You should never use these directories when working on programming projects. Other people can simply take your work without you even knowing it was stolen. You may want to check with your lab administrator or instructor if you are unsure about the status of a public directory on a lab machine.

One of the oldest rackets in the computer lab is the acquisition of printouts from either the trash or the public printer. Take your old printouts home with you to toss in the recycle bin or at the very least take them elsewhere in the building for disposal. Cheaters also prefer to simply pick up nice, new copies of assignments as they are printing out. The moral is to keep up with your work and make sure you are not providing someone an opportunity to get him- or herself and you both in hot water with your instructor, trying to explain who copied whom.

Theft

Computer labs are also locations ripe for your personal possessions to be stolen. If you are using Zip disks, be careful about leaving them in the drives. They can be carried away in a second with your hard work on them.

Take great care with laptops, CDs, and other personal equipment you may be handling in the lab. If you walk away to get a printout, someone may simply walk away with your laptop. Thieves are also after your work and may take action to get it beyond simple plagiarism. Disks, laptops, and CDs are often stolen in pursuit of a working source code.

Malicious Mischief

Hackers and pranksters love to target novice users with harmless, and sometimes not so harmless, mischief. Any sort of suspicious actions you notice should be reported. Novice programmers often have their files erased or changed around by hackers in the lab. It is very frustrating when you have spent 50 hours developing an assignment and someone decides to delete the file for fun while you were out getting more coffee. Always protect your files and keep them away from public access. Most people of the hacker persuasion prefer to target easy access type files.

Real World

Learning to practice good security habits in college is useful preparation for the corporate environment where theft and mischief cost companies millions of dollars each year. Companies expend great effort and resources to protect their source code.

4

The Compiling and Debugging Process

You will find that creating the source code file is the simplest part of creating the application. The challenges start when you attempt to compile your source code (create the executable file) for the first time. If you are like most programmers, your source code will contain errors and other problems that you will have to fix before the executable can be created. You may find that even though you followed all the rules, you still have problems with the way the program operates. This chapter focuses on the conversion of your source code into an executable file. It also provides you with some exercises to get you started on this process.

Compiling Files

The Compile Process

Once you have created a source code file, you can attempt to compile it into an object file. Most programmers, particularly beginning programmers, will spend a great deal of time at this stage deciphering error messages and making corrections to source code. In the earlier chapters, we referred to the object file, which was created from the source code and resulted in a machine language file that could be "linked" into the library of C++ instructions. This is the first step in the process of compilation.

We will pick up at the end of the tutorial from Chapter 3 where we created the myProj project and the myFirstCpp file. This program should work, but you may have made typographical errors when you typed it into the editor and those typos will cause errors to happen when you compile the program. Let's walk through a quick compile so that you can see whether you typed the program exactly or made some minor mistakes. We'll use this experience as a guideline for our discussion of errors.

The easiest way to get back into the myFirstCpp program is to simply open the netFun subdirectory and double left-click on the folder for the project myProj. When you open the subdirectory, you should see Figure 4.1.

Figure 4.1
The netFun
Subdirectory

If you don't see the file or were not able to type it in, you can retrieve the project from the disk included with this book. You could certainly choose to edit the myFirstCpp file directly, but you should use the project. This is done by double-clicking the project icon (myProj). After you double left-click on the myProj icon, Visual C++ opens and your source code appears in the main window, as shown in Figure 4.2.

Figure 4.2
Open Project

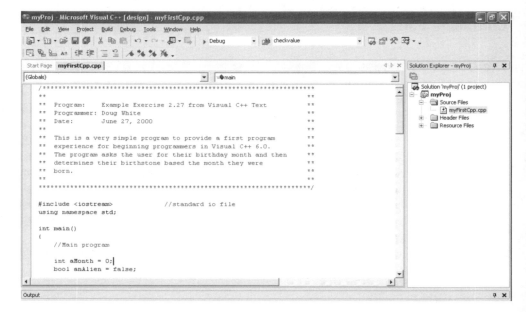

Scan the source code for obvious errors before attempting to compile the code the first time. Proofreading helps you to avoid those long lists of errors that are so frustrating to beginning programmers. However, because you are just starting out, you may not recognize the errors initially. When you have a little more experience, you should definitely make this a practice.

You should now attempt to create an object file from your source code and see how well you did with the typing. There are several paths to this goal in Visual C++. All of the compile options are in the **Build** menu. Click on the **Build** menu and you should see something like Figure 4.3. The easiest option here is to choose **Build Solution** (or press F7). This compiles and links all the files in the project. The **Compile** option merely compiles this individual file. The difference allows you to control the process when you are developing more complicated (multi-file) projects. For now, choose **Build Solution** or press F7 and you should see something like Figure 4.4. **1 Succeeded** indicates the compile and link process was completed without any errors. If you have errors in the source code due to typos, the message will look like Figure 4.5. In this example, the user has received seven build error messages and no warning messages. Now we will discuss these problems and how to approach correcting them.

Figure 4.3
Build Menu

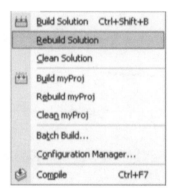

Figure 4.4
Succeeded

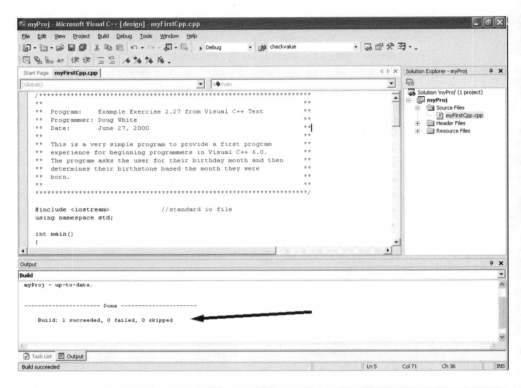

Figure 4.5
Error Messages

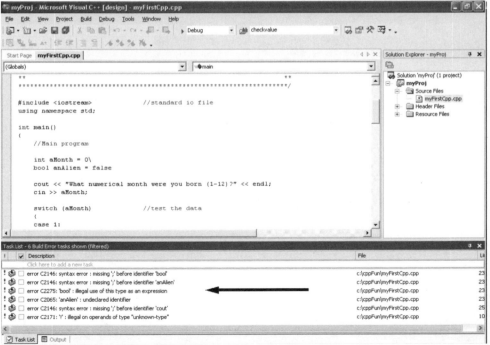

Syntax and Logic Errors

All of the errors you deal with in programming fall into two categories: **logic errors** and **syntax errors**. As a beginning programmer, you will encounter many of each type. Learning to get rid of them is as much an art as a science. We may compare learning to program with learning to play a musical instrument. When you first start it's frustrating because you can't play even a simple song that the instructor plays easily. The only solution is practice, practice, practice. Over time, you will develop shortcuts to solving problems and you will begin to develop strategies for approaching the most complex issues. This is one of the reasons that programmers traditionally were required to take a lot of math. While you may never have to take a derivative in real life, the process of working through a calculus problem is very similar to the process used to solve a programming problem.

Definition 4.1

A *syntax error* is simply a violation of the rules of a language. Much as the use of the word "ain't" is considered a violation of the syntax of English, the misuse of structure and form in programming is a violation of the compiler's rules. Both can result in missed communication and a halt in the process you desire.

When the initial compile takes place, the compiler carefully looks at each instruction in your code and compares it to what it knows and what has been defined by the programmer. For each instruction that is unknown, an error occurs. Beginning programmers encounter many syntax errors since they essentially are writing in an unfamiliar language. This might equate to trying to write a paper in German or Spanish instead of your native language. Most of us make many grammatical and spelling errors in our own language; when we try another, the problem is even worse.

The more complicated problems begin when you are successful in actually compiling the source code and the program doesn't behave as expected. This can be devastating if you are developing commercial applications. Your company would be very embarrassed when the product results in a constant parade of calls from users wanting to know why myFirstCpp crashed again. Even worse would be the case of a program that doesn't do what was expected but continues to function.

This type of problem is called a logic error. Logic errors manifest themselves in strange ways. One of the oldest acronyms in computer science is GIGO, which stands for garbage in, garbage out. Programmers must be on guard to eliminate logic errors, as they will likely be blamed if the program results in catastrophe.

Definition 4.2

A *logic error* is a mistake that complies with the rules of the compiler. It may take the form of a misentered value, a mathematical expression that is coded incorrectly, or some other form. This type of error is very dangerous and is difficult to detect without a great deal of testing.

Unlike syntax errors, which are detected by the compiler, logic errors may go undetected until the program is processed using test data or, even worse, until the application is released! Later in this chapter, we will discuss some strategies for detecting logic errors during development.

Real World

Imagine that a programmer is writing a program to print payroll checks for hourly workers and one of the inputs the programmer uses is the hourly wage for a Type 7 employee (whatever that is). Now, suppose the wage is supposed to be input as \$15.25 per hour but instead the wage is input as \$15.52 per hour, a common mistake called a transposition. Each week Bill, a Type 7 employee, makes \$620.80 instead of \$610.00 if he works 40 hours. The problem may go unnoticed for a long time. After eight weeks, Bill would have been over-paid \$86.40; after 52 weeks, \$561.60. Imagine the company has 700 Type 7 employees who are all overpaid for one year. A \$393,120.00 deficit will be revealed when the books are audited and guess who will be to blame?

Another real-world example would be of creating an application to compute the meters of steel need-ed to build a bridge across the Hudson River. Suppose an engineer uses the program, and the calculation is off due to rounding or some other mathematical error. When the bridge is built, it fails to cross the river by 100 centimeters. Try to imagine the resulting litigation.

Initial Syntax Errors

When you run the first compile, you will likely receive a number of syntax errors. In fact, you may receive a large number of syntax errors. Let's return to our earlier source code. As a second illustration of the com-pile process, suppose we corrected some of the syntax errors in the code and pressed the **Compile** button; we would see the screen shown in Figure 4.6.

In the task list window (see the arrow in Figure 4.6, we now see seven error messages. The compile failed due to syntax errors in the source code. The programmer will now have to try to debug the source code.

Figure 4.6
Syntax Error
Messages

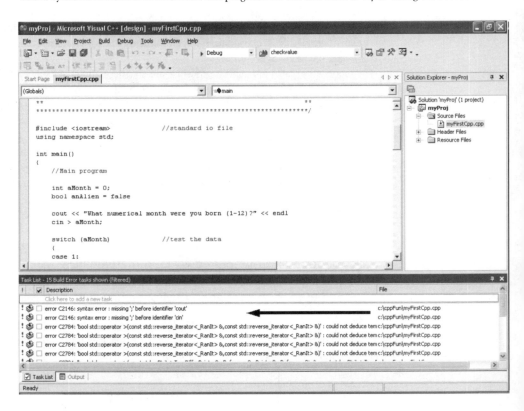

The Art of Debugging

Debugging is an art form and some programmers are better at it than others. All programmers, regardless of their level of experience, must practice debugging. Through practice, programmers become good at solving these problems.

First, it is helpful to develop a plan for debugging the source code. This can save you a great of deal of time and allows you to proceed in a logical fashion. Beginning programmers need all the help they can get on the problems they encounter. A set of steps, like the one outlined here, could help you in your problem-solving endeavors. Your instructor may suggest alternative procedures.

Eight steps to debug a problem:

1. Proofread before compiling.
2. Compile.
3. Correct the obvious errors in a single pass.
4. Recompile.
5. Repeat Steps 3 and 4 until no further errors are obvious.
6. Attempt to solve the remaining errors in a top-down fashion.
7. Solve whatever errors you can without spending long periods of time on any given error.
8. Recompile whenever you feel you don't see any further solutions.

Step 1: Proofread before compiling.

The worst experience for students is to run that first compile when they feel happy about what they have accomplished and 100 to 1000 errors occur. It makes the task ahead seem insurmountable. Scan your code once before you compile and fix anything you see. You certainly shouldn't try to find every single error because the compiler is a helpful tool to point out errors, but you should try to fix what you can see easily before you press that button.

Step 2: Compile.

This is the first compile and should result in quite a few errors unless you did a lot of upfront planning and proofing.

Step 3: Correct the obvious errors in a single pass.

Once you have run that first compile and have obtained a significant number of errors, you have to proceed according to plan. A single syntax error may cause the compiler to believe numerous other syntax errors are occurring. For instance, let's say you mistyped **ofo** when you defined the identifier **foo** in your program. If you then use **foo** 1500 times in the source code, you will have at least 1500 errors in your program. Thus, you could correct the single error and remove 1500 syntax errors.

Look at the error lines and if you see the error, fix it. Otherwise leave it for later. It may vanish when you correct something else. Don't worry too much at this point about things you don't recognize.

One handy feature in Visual C++ is the ability to jump from the error message to the line on which the compiler believes the error occurred. Double-clicking the error message moves the cursor to the line where the compiler detected the error. This is the way to locate all the possible error lines in the code quickly. Remember though, just because an error message has occurred on a given line does not mean there is actually an error on that line. If the error is not obvious to you, leave it, and go to the next error in the list.

Step 4: Recompile.

Now, you should recompile the source code with the corrections. Hopefully, you will have fewer errors, but don't be alarmed if you suddenly have a lot more. Some syntax errors can mask many other errors or even cause the compilation to stop. This is nothing to be alarmed about, just part of the process.

Step 5: Repeat until no further errors are obvious.

Repeat the first two steps and fix all the obvious errors until you can't find any more solutions. This may take many repeats or it may take only a few, depending on the errors and your level of expertise.

Step 6: Attempt to solve the remaining errors in top-down fashion.

Now, the hard part, fixing errors when you don't see the immediate problem. In this case one of two things is probably to blame: (1) an error that you don't recognize, or (2) an error that you recognize is causing a problem you didn't expect it to cause, and the compiler is not smart enough understand.

The newer you are to programming, the more errors you will have never seen and thus, the more situations will occur in which you don't know the immediate answer. As you practice, you will get used to certain types of errors and they will need simple fixes, but you will see puzzling occurrences no matter how long you have been programming. Thus, you need a strategy for solving problems.

Work from the beginning of the program, because in most compilers, the errors are detected from the beginning, sequentially, until the end. Some errors are so severe the compiler will simply refuse to continue.

First, assume your syntax is wrong and verify that you have input the keyword or other elements in the appropriate manner. For C++ syntax, look up the command in a reference book like Gaddis, even if you think it's right. This will help you learn the syntax and verify that your instructions are correct.

You should also add comments, called working comments, to the corrections. This will help you remember what you have changed and how you have changed it. You can use block comments to do this and you might consider numbering them so that you can refer to the numbers later, as in Example 4.1.

Example 4.1

....

The Block Comment Checklist

```
cuot << "This is a line of code" << endl;
/***********Debug*****************
1)      Error is undeclared identifier
2)      Checked syntax for literal
3)      Checked syntax for screen output
a.      Cuot is misspelled
*/
```

This is a simple example, but if you start listing things, it will really help you to work through the debug process. Obviously, before you turn in your source code, you should remove this type of commenting unless you were unable to remove the error. Then your instructor will be able to see how you tried to solve the problem and may be able to quickly identify what the problem is and provide feedback.

We need a set of steps to attempt to figure out what the problem may be when it is more complex than just a misspelled word. Following is a set of steps for general debugging. The more uncomfortable you feel about the problem, the more a set of structured steps will help you solve it.

Example 4.2

The General Debugging Checklist

1. *Visually verify spelling and case of keywords and identifiers.*
2. *Verify syntax with a reference book, not just visually.*
3. *Try to find an example in the reference book that does something similar and compare it to your code.*
4. *Verify that the delimiters used for that line are there.*
5. *Without looking at your source code or notes, rewrite the instruction on a piece of paper and then compare it to your source code (don't cheat).*
6. *Verify that the line is really the source of the error by commenting the line out using //. Be advised that many other errors may result from doing this, but just worry about the current line and current error for now.*

Real World

Structured steps to solving problems will always help. Consider airline pilots. Their jobs are critical, and a tiny mistake can result in catastrophe. Pilots always use checklists for everything. Next time you get on a plane and the cabin door is open, notice that the pilots have checklists on their laps as they preflight the plane. Even in small single-engine planes, pilots use checklists and you will typically find they have a check-list for all the normal procedures and all the possible emergencies. This helps them to make sure that they checked everything and that they use logic, even when they are in an emergency. Programmers get frustrated and tired. They spend long hours trying to solve complex problems. Use a checklist to debug problems and you won't forget anything.

Step 1: Visually verify spelling and case of keywords and identifiers.

Misspelling and using the wrong case are common causes of problems. You should quickly review the spelling of keywords. Make sure they appear in blue. If your keywords appear in blue, they are being con-sidered keywords by the compiler. Likewise, make sure your literals and identifiers are not blue or green (indicating they are comments). You should also make sure your identifiers are spelled correctly. As I sug-gested earlier, write down the line of code on paper and then compare all the identifiers back to where they are defined. This technique is particularly helpful if you are having problems with spelling and can't seem to spot the errors. Many beginning programmers have great difficulty spotting spelling errors, particularly in non-standard usage where the words and phrases they are typing are unfamiliar.

Step 2: Verify syntax with a reference book, not just visually.

You should always make sure the syntax is correct, even if your eyes tell you that it is. It is often the case that you glance at something and assume that it is correct and, therefore, miss the problem. As with the spelling problem, you should write the phrase down on a piece of paper and then compare it to a reference book. This forces you to think about the problem and to review it carefully.

Step 3: Try to find an example in the reference book that does something similar and compare it to your code.

Many programmers love to work by example and the more expertise you have, the more you will be able to use this tactic. Find an example and then see if you can figure out where your code differs from the example. If a lot of the code is similar, it may point you to the exact location of the error. Certainly, there are occasions where this does not work, or you simply cannot find an example, but if you can find something similar that works, then you have a window into the problem.

Step 4: Verify that the delimiters used for that line are there.3

Delimiters certainly can cause problems. You may want to verify the delimiters on the lines above and below the error line as they can sometimes cause errors. Visual C++ has proven reliable at detecting missing delimiters, but as you will see in some later examples, a missing delimiter can cause a very confusing error earlier and/or later in the program. Typically, the errors occur after the missing delimiter.

Step 5: Without looking at your source code or notes, rewrite the instruction on a piece of paper and then compare it to your source code.

This approach helps you to try a second time to write the instruction. You may do something dramatically different in the second version that will tip you off to the error. Students write lines of code when they are distracted or thinking of some other approach, and when they rewrite it later, they use a different approach that helps them solve the error. The critical message here is to not look at the original, problematic source code. If you do that, you will likely just copy down what you already have, and this step becomes a pointless exercise.

Step 6: Verify that the line is really the source of the error by commenting the line out with //.

This is a common technique programmers use to work with code in the debugging process. The programmer comments the line out where the error is occurring and then recompiles the code to see what happens. A variety of results may occur and you shouldn't be alarmed if your program suddenly jumps from 5 errors to 50. Many errors may be caused by the omission of a declaration or other important statement in your source code. Don't worry though; this simply gives you a chance to work with the line in question.

One possible outcome is that the error simply disappears. This is a nice result, since it implies that the error is being caused by the line you are examining. This tells you that you may want to fall back on some of the previous techniques again until you spot exactly what the error is.

A second outcome is that the error moves to the next line. This would imply that the error might be caused by an earlier line of code. In particular, these types of clues often point to missing delimiters preceding the line on which you are working. Remember that the compiler is not very smart. Don't take its recommendation at face value.

The most important thing the beginning programmer needs to remember is that it takes a great deal of time to resolve all the syntax errors you make. The second most important lesson is that the compiler cannot be trusted to point you in the right direction. On the simplest of errors, the compiler will always be correct, but as errors become more convoluted, the compiler may make many mistakes with its limited intelligence. Don't be afraid to experiment with comments and other changes to the code to see what happens. Debugging is largely detective work. As you develop your own bag of tricks, you will find it becomes easier.

Philosophy

You should adopt the philosophy "Never make a change you cannot explain." Beginning programmers often feel a sense of desperation setting in about three o'clock in the morning on the day a program is due. This may result in trying desperate things, like sticking in semi-colons or curly braces in response to error messages. You must understand why you are doing something. If you can't explain why you just added that semi-colon, then don't do it. Consult your reference books to determine why a semi-colon should or should not go in that location. If you fail to follow this philosophy, you will just create larger problems by random actions.

The second part of the philosophy is "Never trust an error message." All too often beginning programmers encounter an error message such as:

```
Missing ; on line 701
```

The natural response is to double-click the message, jump to line 701 and insert a delimiter. I have often looked at programs that have lines like this:

```
AFunCall(x);;;;;;
```

This results from the programmer getting frantic and continuing to get missing ; messages on the line. Never ever start down this path to the dark side of programming. Always make sure you understand why the error message occurred. Do not rely on random actions to correct problems or you will end up with a large mess instead of a source code.

Simple Debugging Tutorial

In an effort to provide you with some practice debugging Visual C++ syntax, a sample program is included here to get you started. You may wish to work through this tutorial after you have started working on your first assignment in Visual C++.

Step 1: Create a subdirectory.

You should create a subdirectory on your hard drive, floppy disk, or Zip disk to store the file we will be working with in the tutorial. Name this subdirectory tutorial. To create the subdirectory, complete the following steps:

1.   Open the Microsoft Explorer using the **Windows** key and **e**. You should see something like Figure 4.7.

Figure 4.7
Creating a
Subdirectory for
the Tutorial

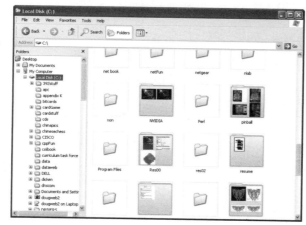

Figure 4.8
The C Drive

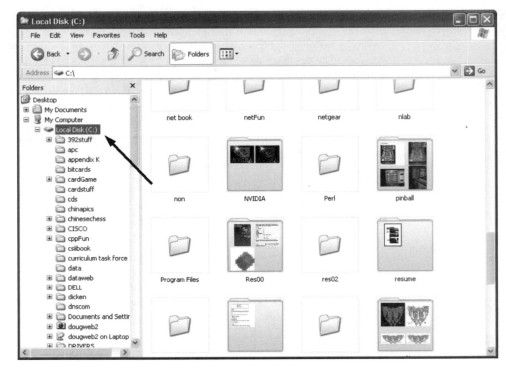

2. Click on the drive on which you wish to create the tutorial. Figure 4.8 shows the C drive.
3. Open the File menu and choose New and Folder, as shown in Figure 4.9.

Figure 4.9
The New Folder

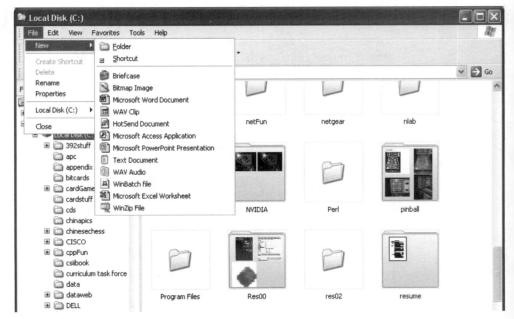

Figure 4.10
The New Folder
Exists

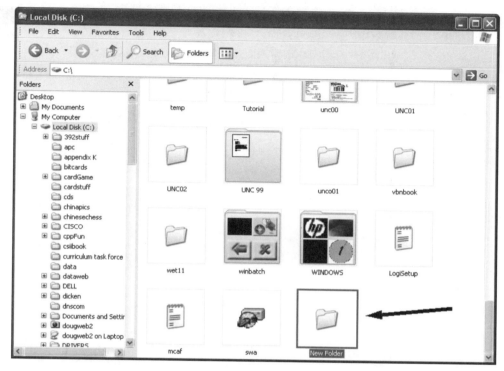

4. The new folder should appear at the bottom of the screen and be named New Folder, as shown in Figure 4.10.

5. Rename the new folder by typing **Tutorial**, as shown in Figure 4.11 (this assumes there is no other folder on your disk named tutorial).

Figure 4.11
Rename the
Folder

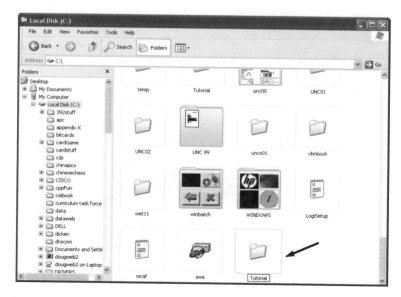

Figure 4.12 The Saved File

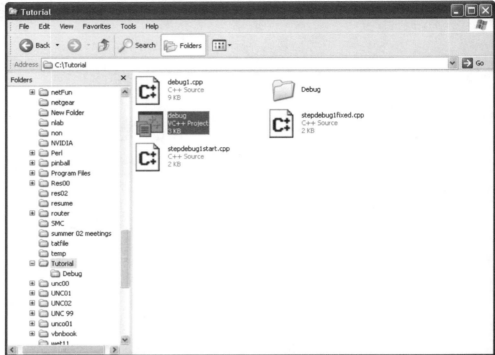

6. Now download the project file **debug** from the floppy disk and save it into the folder you just created, as shown in Figure 4.12.

Step 2: Open the Program File in Visual C++.

1. Double-click the project folder. It should open to display the project file, debug, as shown in Figure 4.13.

Figure 4.13 The Project File

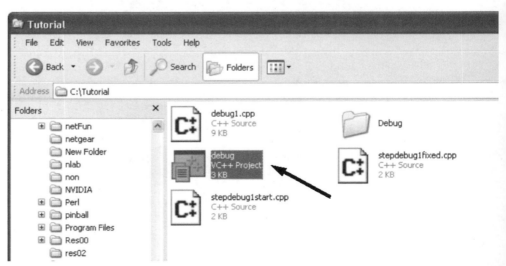

2. Double-click the project file to open the project in Visual C++. This should look like Figure 4.14.

Figure 4.14
The Open Project

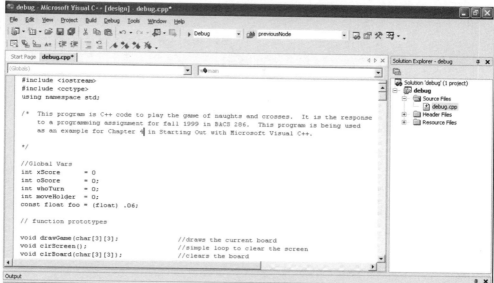

Step 3: Run an Initial Compile.

Now, you need to begin your first debugging session with Visual C++. This tutorial contains a number of simple syntax errors to help you get a feel for what is going on in the debugging process so that you can begin to develop your skill using the steps outlined previously.

1. Press **F7** to start the build process.
2. You will see the compile run, and two errors should appear in the lower window. They are shown in Figure 4.15.
3. Now, double-click on the first error to jump to that line of the program. The error is:

```
c:\Tutorial\debug1.cpp(13): error C2144: syntax error : 'int' should be preceded by ';'
```

which indicates that there is a missing semi-colon (delimiter) somewhere on that line. In this case, the compiler actually tells you that the missing delimiter is before the keyword **int**. This means that the error is not actually on this line but before it. This is shown in Figure 4.16.

As you practice debugging, errors like this will become easy to spot and repair.

4. Correct the error by adding the semi-colon on the line:

```
int xScore        = 0;
```

5. Save the source code by pressing **File**, **Save All**.
6. Recompile the source code by pressing the **F7** button again.
7. Uh oh, now you have more errors instead of less (eight to be exact). This is shown in Figure 4.17.

    In the earlier compile, some error caused the compile to stop. Sometimes the compiler simply cannot deal with errors and is forced to discontinue compiling at that point. That has happened here. The good news is that several of these error messages may be caused by a single error. This is why we want to work from the top down in the program.

Figure 4.15
The First Two
Errors

Figure 4.16
The Missing
Delimiter

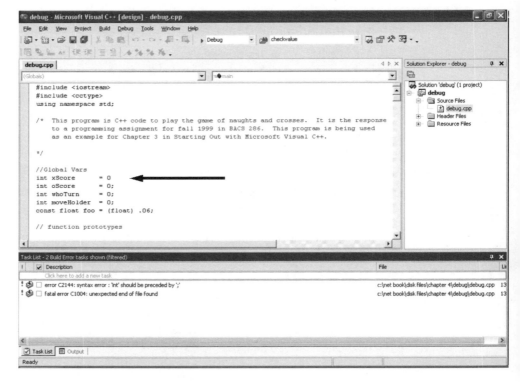

Figure 4.17
Eight Errors

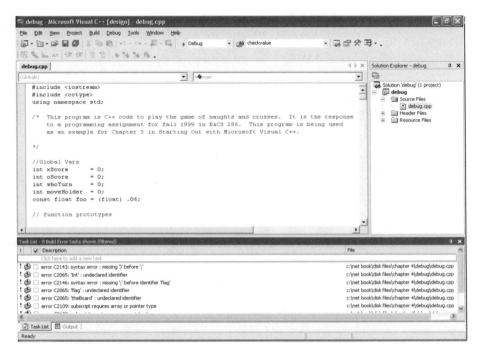

8. Double-click on the first error and let's see where it is, as shown in Figure 4.17.

```
c:\Tutorial\debug1.cpp(19): error C2143: syntax error : missing ')' before ';'
```

The message implies there is a missing close parenthesis on this line somewhere. You should always remember that if you open a parenthesis, you have to close it. If you look carefully at the line, you will see there is no closing parenthesis on it. You may also have no idea where the parenthesis should go if you are unfamiliar with the syntax. If you are unsure, the worst thing you can do is to just start adding parentheses trying to get rid of the error. The message implies the parenthesis should appear before the delimiter, so let's assume you look up the syntax for this statement and realize the parentheses should appear between the square bracket (]) and the delimiter (;).

9. Add the parenthesis, save, and recompile with the **F7** button. The result is shown in Figure 4.18.

10. Let's look at the next error. Double-click to jump to the line:

```
c:\Tutorial\debug1.cpp(42): error C2065: 'Int' : undeclared identifier
```

This is an undeclared identifier error. These are very common errors that all programmers deal with every time they write programs. The error usually means a misspelled word, a typo, or something similar. These errors often cause many additional errors because if the identifier is not defined, every one of its occurrences in the program will result in an error message. Again, you need to look closely at the line to see what is wrong. The message says **Int** is undeclared. We will assume you know that **Int** is supposed to be a keyword so it should be blue, but it's not! Look up the syntax for the **int** keyword in a reference book. You realize that **int** cannot have a capital "I" in front of it or it's not a keyword. This is an important lesson to remember for C++: the case of everything matters. Case errors may be something very simple as an identifier x not being equal to X in C++.

Figure 4.18
Seven Errors Left

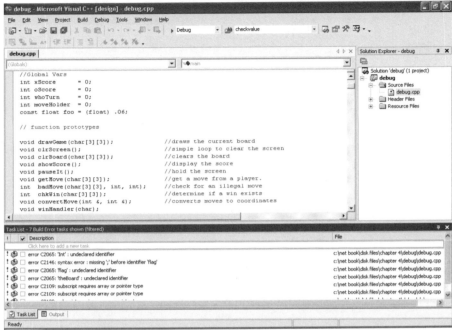

11. Correct the Int error by changing I to i, save, and recompile. The result is shown in Figure 4.19. Well, that got rid of some more errors and left us with only four. You see that some of the later errors are echoes of the case error. This is an argument in favor of the top-down approach.

Figure 4.19
The Corrected
Int Error

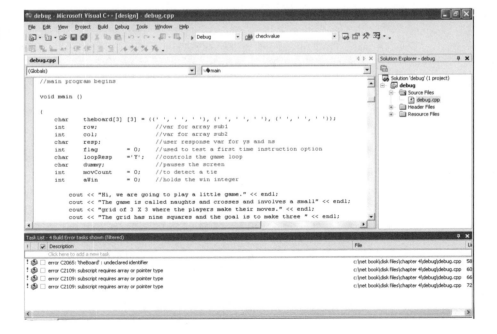

12. Double-click on the next error and look at the line:

```
c:\Tutorial\debug1.cpp(57): error C2065: 'theBoard' : undeclared identifier
```

Now, you should see Figure 4.20.

Figure 4.20
Line 57 Error

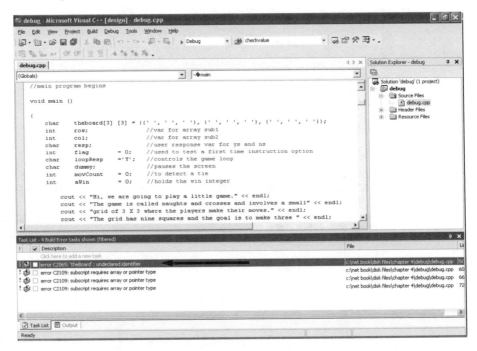

This is a function call, which may be unfamiliar to you. Again, you may look up the syntax for a function call, and if you do, you will find that the format is correct. The message implies that `theBoard` is undeclared. You may or may not be aware that this is not a declaration, but merely a usage of the name (identifier) `theBoard`. Thus, the error must be in the declaration or in the local usage on this line. The most common reason for this type of error is a misspelled name or the misuse of case. Look back to the declaration of `theBoard` as shown in Figure 4.21.

You should see that the declaration is `theboard` not `theBoard`. Here, you have to make a judgment call about which is incorrect, the declaration or the use on line 57. If you wrote the source code, you should know what conventions you have used for naming identifiers, but you may sometimes be looking at someone else's source code. Quickly scan the program and see if there are other occurrences of `theboard` or `theBoard`.[1]

You immediately see repeated usage of `theBoard` and no other usage of `theboard`. This implies that `theBoard` is likely the correct declaration.

---

[1]Note that C++ will allow the use of both `theboard` and `theBoard`, as well as any other variant, considering them different identifiers. This is a poor practice and serves to confuse the programmer, the analyst, and anyone else trying to review the source code. Nevertheless, you should be aware that it may be done and take care to avoid multiple declarations. In this program, you will not find a second declaration.

Figure 4.21
Declaration

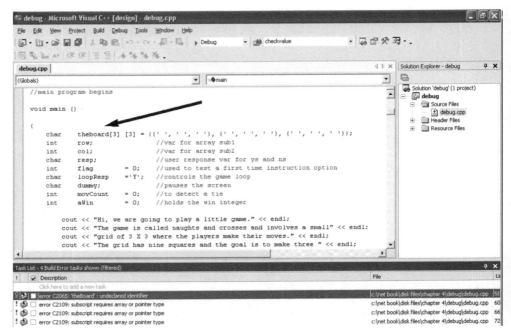

13. Change the declaration line from `theboard` to `theBoard`, save, and recompile. The result is shown in Figure 4.22.

    Wow! All of the errors are gone. This is a classic example of a single error resulting in many additional problems.

Figure 4.22
Errors Resolved

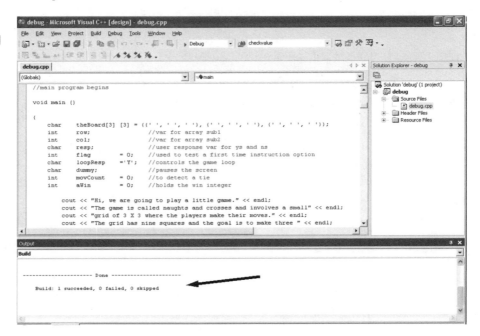

This concludes the tutorial on basic syntax debugging. You should remember to follow the steps outlined earlier when you attempt this with your own program.

Common Syntax Errors

In this section, an initial discussion of syntax errors and on the level of beginning programmers is introduced. The reader should understand that it is not possible to illustrate every conceivable error, nor is it possible to describe all of the circumstances that generate errors. Instead, the goal is to reveal errors that are very common among first-time programmers and to show how these errors occur and how to resolve them in your programs. The assumption of this section is that you are actually to the point of working on your programs in Visual C++ and have some experience now with syntax. This book does not attempt to describe C++ syntax, and you should refer to your course materials or *Starting Out with C++* by Tony Gaddis for references to C++ syntax and programming.

In each section of the error discussion, I will provide you with a general discussion of the type of error (that could apply to most any language), an example showing the error in Visual C++, and the error number and statement from the Visual C++ compiler. Remember, not all errors are covered, merely common errors that occur with great frequency for beginning programmers.

The Missing Name (Undeclared Identifier)

One of the errors most commonly encountered by beginning programmers is the misuse of either a keyword or a name the programmer attempted to define (called a variable/identifier). This type of error is common to every programming language but may be described differently by different compilers. The Visual C++ compiler describes it as an undeclared identifier error and is usually able to point directly to the line of the source code where this error is detected. This error is shown in Figure 4.23.

Several things may produce this error:

1. The misspelling of a keyword
2. The misspelling of a programmer defined name (identifier)

Figure 4.23
The Undeclared Identifier

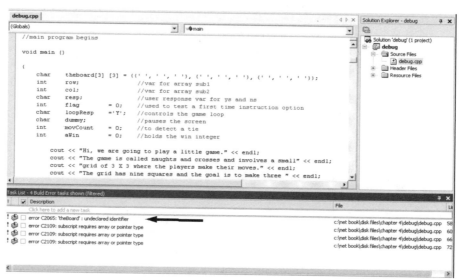

3. The misuse of case in a keyword
4. The misuse of case in an identifier
5. The failure to declare an identifier

In each of the circumstances, the compiler thinks that the programmer has used an identifier that has not been declared. For example, suppose you used a keyword **get**, but instead of using it properly, you input it as GET. Now, remember that Visual C++ is case sensitive and everything is based on ASCII numbers such that get ¹ GET ¹Get ¹ gET and so forth. It is very easy when you are typing to misuse case. If the compiler encounters the keyword GET, it thinks GET is some new identifier the programmer created but forgot to define for the compiler. Thus, a syntax error of the undeclared identifier type occurs.

When you encounter an undeclared identifier error in Visual C++ you should first go to the line where the error occurred and then follow the steps for debugging discussed earlier.

Delimiter Errors

Another common error for all programmers is the misuse or omission of delimiters. Modern programming languages are usually based on delimited phrases instead of the columnar restrictions used in the past. This means that the programmer must tell the compiler where the instruction ends because there is no column or line restriction on the instruction. In Visual C++, the delimiter is the semi-colon (;). Beginning programmers have a lot of difficulty with this because the semi-colon is unfamiliar. Thus, the most common error looks like the following:

```
c:\Tutorial\debug1.cpp(61): error C2146: syntax error : missing ';' before identifier 'pauseIt'
```

The C2146 error, which tells you that there is a missing semi-colon, is very common. Most of the time, this error reflects a problem on the preceding line in the form of a missing delimiter. The real danger for the beginning programmer is to fail to understand the error, the error message, and the action to take. Therefore, make sure you really understand why and where to put the delimiter.

A second type of delimiter error involves the use of braces, brackets, and parentheses in Visual C++. These mistakes can result in complicated errors that are difficult to resolve. Such an error is shown in Figure 4.24.

This error seems to imply there is a problem with the semi-colon delimiter on this line. You must be careful here since removal of the delimiter would be disastrous. This is a tricky error even if you are familiar with the syntax, because it is caused by the lack of a closing brace. For a single line, you should always count the opens and then subtract closes to see if you end up with an equal number. If you have more opens than closes on the line, you have found the problem. In Figure 4.24, it's a missing brace at the end of the line. As a beginning programmer, you may need a lot of time to look up syntax for this type of error. This is another example of the philosophy "Never trust an error message."

Missing closes can result in other horrible messes, as shown in Figure 4.25.

The poor beginning programmer who gets this collection of error messages usually ends up in the instructor's office feeling like there is no solution to this problem. Then the instructor fixes it in about 10 seconds. The real secret here is knowing what to look for in the error log. It's the last message that you should see:

```
C:\Tutorial\debug1.cpp(417): fatal error C1075: end of file found before the left
brace '{' at 'c:\Tutorial\debug1.cpp(34)' was matched
```

Figure 4.24
A Delimiter Error with Braces

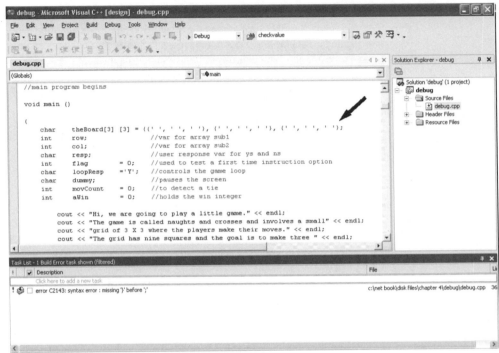

Figure 4.25
A Horrible Mess with Delimiters

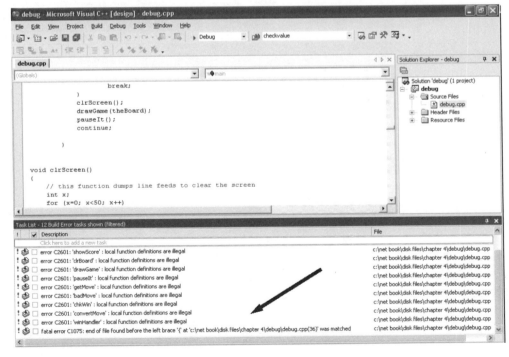

This error message is a huge clue that there is a missing } delimiter or there is an extra delimiter in your file somewhere. It is likely that a lot of the other errors are the result of this one. You will have a difficult time flipping through all the pages of code trying to find all the delimiters and match them up. Even experienced programmers have difficulty with this. You need a method.

Use the outline approach to delimiters. Each time you have an open delimiter, {, put a comment after the delimiter on the line in outline form, // I, // II, and so forth. For each sublevel of delimiter, use the outline approach, //A, //1, //a, and so forth. Then do the same thing when they close, but with small letters, so that the last delimiter in the program, }, should match the outline for the first delimiter. If you don't end up back at //I you have omitted a delimiter, and if you are already at //I before you reach the end, you may have some extras.

Warnings

Most compilers will also provide warnings to the programmer about certain types of actions that may represent problems but do not cause the compiler to flag an error. The inclination of most beginning programmers is to simply ignore warnings since the program will compile even with hundreds of warnings. This is a bad habit and can lead to logic errors and other problems later in the compile process. Resolve warnings as well as errors.

Perhaps the most common warning my students receive is a typecasting warning. This warning can be seen in Figure 4.26.

The compiler issues this type of warning whenever one type of number is converted to another type without the inclusion of a typecasting operation. The best example of such a warning would be an attempt to store the value of π in an integer. π is approximately equal to 3.14... and if this value were moved to an

Figure 4.26
A Typecasting
Warning

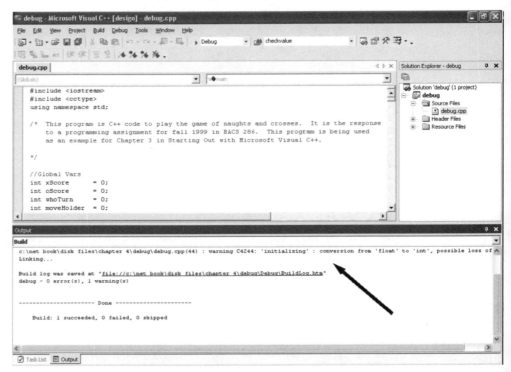

integer it would be truncated by the compiler to 3. This would cause serious logic errors in any output. Thus, in Figure 4.26, it is necessary to perform what is called a typecast operation to notify the compiler that the programmer fully understands what he or she is doing and wants to do it anyway.

Anytime a number is moved from a larger type to a smaller type in Visual C++, a typecasting operation must be performed. (You will learn about other reasons for this operation in your studies of Visual C++.) When you receive a warning similar to that shown in Figure 4.26, you need to investigate and decide if you really do want to typecast a number.

In Figure 4.26, the literal number .06 is being moved into a floating point type identifier in Visual C++. All literals are considered to be double precision types by default, so when this double type is moved into a float type (which has a smaller storage area) there is the potential to lose data. Anyone can see that .06 is not going to lose any data during the move, so a typecast here is perfectly legitimate. Figure 4.27 illustrates the removal of the warning.

As a programmer, you should remember that you should always understand why something is being done and not just react to a warning or error. Doing so can lead you to serious problems that are difficult to detect.

Your instructor may wish to discuss some of the other types of warnings with you. Never be satisfied with a program that is anything less than one hundred percent.

Figure 4.27
The Elimination
of a Typecast
Warning

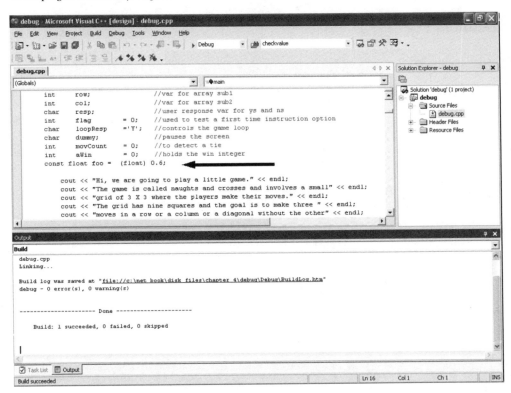

Disk Space Limitations

A final note about the initial compilation process is the disk space limitation. When using Visual C++, it is not uncommon for students to save their work to floppy disks. The standard 3.5-inch floppy disk has 1.44

megabytes of disk space available. This is plenty for storage of most intro level C++ courses' source codes. The problems arise because (1) students save too much work to the same floppy and (2) the project, compiled object, and library files as well as the executable files can take up considerable more space than the source code alone. If the floppy is full or becomes full during the compilation process, the compile will fail and a cryptic error message will be generated.

Many students fail to recognize this problem and spend a lot of time trying to resolve this error. Unfortunately, I cannot tell you how much space is needed for a given source code compile and there are other errors that may occur depending on where in the compile process the overflow happens.

Typing Problems

One other common problem worthy of note is the problem with the **L** key in typing. Many typists learned that typing the small l **(ell)** was much faster than typing a 1 (one) on the number line above the letter keys. These two symbols have different ASCII values and can cause horrendous problems in C++. Be sure to use a **1** (one) when you are doing numerics. **0** (zero) and **O** are also often interchanged, but at least they look different if you study them closely. The **1** (one) and the **l** (ell) look the same, but will cause dramatic differences in your program.

Building Files

With luck and hard work, you will be able to remove all those syntax errors at some point. This leads to a successful compile of the program and the creation of all the files the compiler needs to attempt to build an executable **(.exe)** file that you can run. The bad news is that not all syntax errors are detectable by the compiler. There are errors that do not become apparent until the linker attempts to join all the files together in the .exe. The good news is that the linker will generate an error message to warn you of such problems. The bad news is that these error messages are usually not associated with any given line in the program. The following example in Figure 4.28 compiles just fine, but an error message is generated when a build is attempted on the program.

Figure 4.28
A Linker Error

This error is confusing and you will find that double-clicking on the error message no longer works, because the compiler has approved the source code as complying with the syntax rules of C++. This means you have somehow managed to break the rules without breaking the rules. The best example is to use English as a syntax base. Now, you know a lot of rules and that the words to and two and too are often misused. So, suppose you wrote this sentence:

I want two send to letters too you and you to.

Wow, what a mess. Now, an interesting thing is that most native speakers of English, even your seventh-grade English teacher, could make sense of this sentence despite the misused words. Another interesting thing is that a word processor's spell checker and grammar checker might not indicate any problem with this sentence. Even worse, someone with limited or missing skills in English trying to translate this sentence with a dictionary would likely decide to study ancient Coptic instead of English.

This is an example of a syntax problem that is difficult for linear thought processes (like computers and translators using word-for-word dictionaries) to understand. Slang is another example where syntax may be observed, but direct translation is difficult. If a four-year-old boy came home from pre-school and pronounced "I am a cool cat," the meaning is obscure while the syntax is legitimate.

Most beginning programmers run into some linker errors as they develop code, but fortunately, most of these errors are simple because the code being developed is fairly simple. As you improve your programming skills, you will find that you can generate some complicated linker errors.

When the linking process begins and linker errors occur, the linker will generate messages starting with LNK to inform you that the error is a linking error and involves some action the compiler didn't expect. Note the following code from Figure 4.28.

```
myProj error LNK2019: unresolved external symbol "bool __cdecl getCont(void)" (?getCont@@YA_NXZ) ref-
erenced in function _main myProj fatal error LNK1120: 1 unresolved externals
```

In the case of Figure 4.28, two errors are generated, but they usually are found together. The message is scary to most beginning programmers, because it contains numerous symbols and cryptic references.

If you look carefully, you see **getCont**, a name from the program (refer to Figure 4.28), in this error message. This is a clue that can lead you to the solution of this linker error. The following set of steps can help you work through linker errors. Your instructor may wish to provide additional input on common linker errors encountered in his or her course.

Linker Error Steps

1. Look for clues in the error message with particular regard to lines of source code.
2. Visually examine any line of source code that contains the instruction by using the **Edit**, **Find** command on the menu (type the name into the **Find** box). These steps are shown in Figures 4.29 and 4.30.
3. Click **Find Next** and review each line of the program that contains the phrase. In particular, look for misspelling and case errors.

The real focus for basic errors of this type will be on misspelling and case violations. This is almost always the case with LNK 2019 errors because they refer to a name that is legal, but has no instructions associated with it. There are many other linker errors you may encounter, but this method may help you at least zero in on the lines where these errors are occurring. The bad news is that there may be large numbers of lines that fall into this category. Hopefully, in your beginning programming class, most of the linker errors you encounter will fall into the LNK 2019 type and be resolvable using the error steps above. If you are encountering unusual errors, be sure and point them out to your instructor so he or she can be aware of the problem. It is likely happening to others in the class as well.

Figure 4.29
The Edit, Find
Command

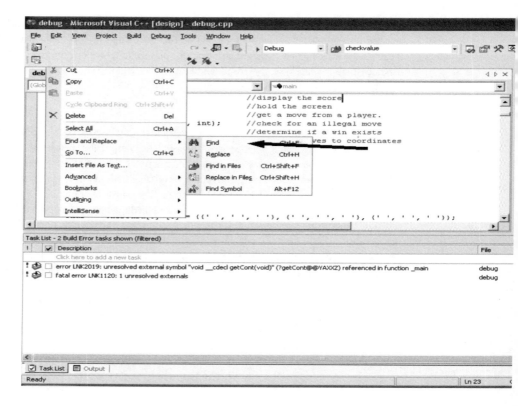

Figure 4.30
The Find Box

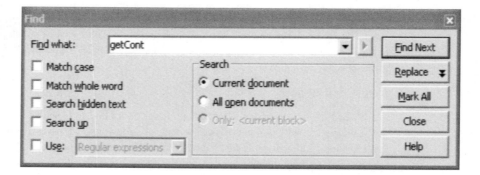

Executing the Program

Finally, you have reached the point where you can smugly click the **Build Solution** button and watch as no errors occur. This is usually accompanied by lots of celebratory dancing and shouts of "Thank you, thank you, thank you." When you have successfully "built a solution" and created the **.exe** file with your program, you can finally proceed to execute the program using the **Debug** menu.

Figure 4.31 shows the **Debug** menu and the **Start without Debugging** option (CTRL-F5). Choose **Start without Debugging** or press **CTRL-F5** to execute the program.

Figure 4.31
Start without
Debugging

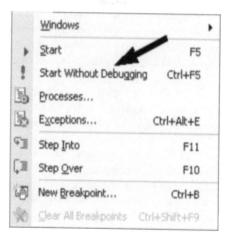

At this point, the program will run correctly or will run and contain logic errors. Many C++ programs run in a DOS window as shown in Figure 4.32.

The DOS window will contain instructions to the user, requests for data, and results of the operations being conducted by the C++ instructions in the source code.

Figure 4.32
The DOS
Execution
Window

Logic Errors

Many beginning programmers feel that when they finally get an **.exe** file built, their job is done and they can go and collect their A on the assignment. Unfortunately, errors can occur here as well. These are called logic errors and are categorized two ways: (1) overt logic errors and (2) covert logic errors.

Overt logic errors are problems in your program where something that is obviously a problem is happening. This is not the same as a syntax or linker error because the program is actually running, but something is still terribly wrong.

Let's use an example of a symphony orchestra. Suppose everyone is playing a Bach concerto except for the trombone player who accidentally got a copy of Dixieland Rag. This can be compared to a syntax error like the one we saw earlier. Now, suppose everyone gets the music straightened out. The trombone player now has a copy of the Bach concerto, but his trombone is badly out of tune. He's playing the right notes, but it's painfully obvious that something is wrong. This is analogous to an overt logic error.

Closer to home, imagine you walk up to an ATM machine and put in all the information to withdraw $20. Suppose the programmer accidentally forgot to have the machine log you out and return your card. This would not cause a syntax or linker error. It is a valid instruction (or lack of an instruction), but it would certainly be an obvious problem.

Covert logic errors are problems in your program that result in less-than-obvious errors. Suppose in our symphony example, the trombone player is now playing the Bach concerto but has received the wrong music and is playing the part written for a bass. The music is correct and it may difficult for someone who is not an expert to figure out what is wrong. In the case of the ATM, imagine that instead of $20 falling into the hopper, $200 falls out but only $20 is deducted from your account. This problem will be difficult to detect even with an accounting audit because there is no record of where the money went.

Spotting an Overt Logic Error

Now that your program is running, you should be able to spot strange occurrences just by working with it. As you practice programming, you will learn to spot problems and anomalous behavior, but even experienced programmers sometimes miss problems. Learn to look for strange things. Try different approaches to running your code that will force these errors to reveal themselves to you instead of to an end-user who has purchased your program. In Chapter 5, the Step Debugger is introduced to help you work through both overt and covert logic errors in your code.

Chapter 4 Exercises

1. Return to the **myFirstCpp** program you created in Chapter 3 and compile and execute it. If you are lucky there will be no errors, but you will probably encounter some. See if you can remove them all using the methods described in this chapter.

2. Get the project **debug2** from the floppy disk and work on this file. There are many syntax errors in this program for you to work on and remove. If you can remove them all, you will have started to develop some real debugging skills for syntax.

3. Try and create some errors on your own. Use the **debug1** program you used for the tutorial in this chapter. See if you can create all the errors intentionally. This will give you some experience with the different types of errors and what they look like in a program.

5 Using the Step Debugger

All programmers experience errors, all of them. All programmers must deal with logic errors, all of them. Overt and covert logic errors are the bane of all programmers' lives, because they are difficult to detect and even more difficult to resolve. Logic errors may be the result of an incorrect value (for instance, $\pi = 3$ instead of 3.14...) or a source code that calls the wrong process at the wrong time (like turning on the heat instead of the air conditioning). The larger the project, the more difficult it is to narrow down where these problems originate.

One of the best tools for uncovering these logic errors and for testing to make sure the problems are non-existent, is the Step Debugger. This tool allows programmers to execute their code one line at a time and even allows for looking at the values of variables, and so forth, during the pause. This powerful tool will enable you to locate problems and correct them.

Unfortunately, the Step Debugger cannot help you with syntax problems. It requires that an executable file be created before the debugger will run. Thus, you will have to resort to the measures discussed in Chapter 3 and Chapter 4 to resolve all the other problems before you can deal with any logic errors that may be plaguing you.

Step Execution

For this chapter, we will first be working with a project called **stepdebug1**. Create a new subdirectory called **step** on your hard drive. You should copy it from the book disk into this subdirectory.

The **stepdebug1.cpp** source code contains some errors that will be good examples in the Step Debugger process. You may wish to wait for your instructor to assign this chapter because it involves more advanced programming concepts that you may not understand on day one (or even day 10). You might also refer to your C++ textbook for references to this material.

Step Debugging Tutorial Part I

1. Open the **stepdebug1** project you saved on your disk.
2. You should see the project with the source code **stepdebug.cpp**, just as in the previous tutorials.
3. First, compile the program by pressing the **Build, Build Solution** item.
4. The program should compile without any errors or warnings (see Figure 5.1).

Figure 5.1
Compiling the
Program

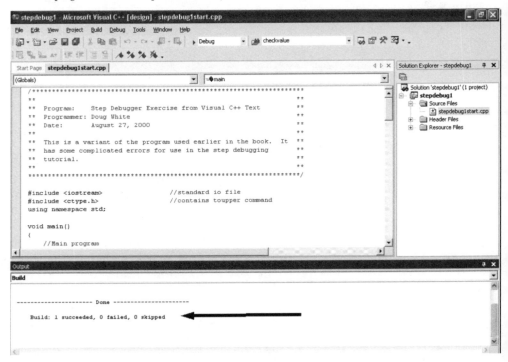

5. Run the program with **Debug, Start without Debugging**. You should see that nothing happens (see Figure 5.2).

Figure 5.2
Program Runs

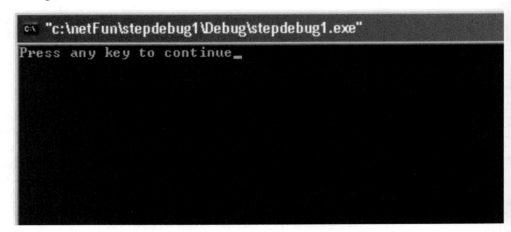

6. Press the space bar or **Return** to continue. You should return to the Visual C++ editing window.
7. The program must have at least one logic error. It doesn't do what you expected. Thus, the best approach is to use the Step Debugger to see what is happening in the program.
8. Click on the **Debug** menu, and **Step Into** (or **F11**) your program (see Figure 5.3).
9. This will actually start the program running but will only execute the first line (see Figure 5.4).

Figure 5.3
Running the
Debugger

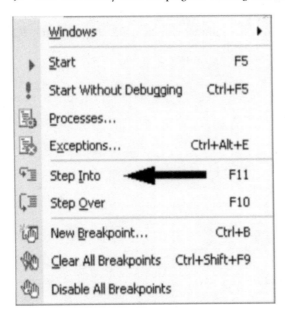

Figure 5.4
Running and
Line Indicator

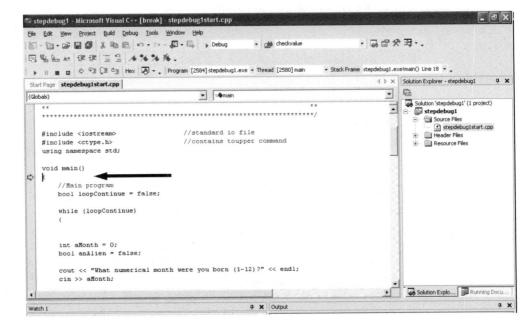

You need to use Step Into at this point since you have no breakpoints in the code. You will see a small yellow arrow, which indicates the next line of code that will be executed. The debugger will go ahead and take care of any preprocessing (includes) and skip into the main program.

The Stepping Options

The Debug menu has several options for stepping through the program (see Figure 5.5).

The five main options that you will use are **Continue**, **Step Into**, **Step Over**, **Step Out**, and **Stop Debugging**.

Figure 5.5
The Debugger
Stepping
Options

Continue (F5)

The **Continue** option tells the debugger to run. This means that if you have no breakpoints in the code, the program will run to its completion. Use this option when you have set some breakpoints in the program and want to get to them (or between them) quickly.

Step Into (F11)

This is a more complex option that allows the programmer to enter a function or other scope instead of just processing through it. If you are working through a program that has function calls, or if you want to see what is happening inside the function, you must use the **Step Into** or the function will simply execute and you will be on the line following the function call in the main program. Basically, any call that places the cursor outside of "main" will require **Step Into** if you want to see the underlying function. This is handy if you want to skip a function you know works, particularly functions included with the compiler. If the line is not a function call, **Step Into** just executes the current line and moves to the next. Don't use this command except to enter your own functions because it is very easy to end up in the C++ substrata, which will be confusing. If you do end up in the C++ functions, just press **Shift-F11**, which will return you to main.

Step Over (F10)

You use this item most in the debugger as it just steps "over" the current line. This doesn't keep the line from executing, just steps over it. It also executes functions calls and other scopes without showing you all the underlying steps that are used to run the function.

Step Out (Shift-F11)

Step Out is the opposite of **Step Into**. If you find yourself in a function or the C++ substrata and don't want to be there, just press **Shift-F11** and you will return to the portion of the code that called the function. The remainder of the function will execute, you just won't see it all happen. This is useful if you think a function may be causing problems and after a few steps realize this is not the source. **Step Out** will also run the program to the end if you press it while in main.

Stop Debugging (Shift-F5)

This command ends the debugging session without executing any further lines of code. Often, as you make a change in the source code, you will want to recompile and re-execute the program. Use **Stop Debugging** to end the session so you can start again.

Inserting and Removing Breakpoints

Before you use the step debugger, you may want to review the source code to try and identify the general area in which the errors are occurring. Breakpoints allow you to get to interesting pieces of the code quickly without stepping a line at a time through hundreds of lines of source code that are not of interest. The tutorial will show you how to insert and remove some breakpoints in the stepdebug1 program. Remember that breakpoints have no impact on your program other than how it executes in the debugger, so don't worry about using them or deleting them at will.

Breakpoints are inserted by right-clicking the mouse on the line where you want to insert or remove the breakpoint. A right-click will open the **Debugger** menu (see Figure 5.6) and allow you to manipulate breakpoints on this line of the source code.

You can tell when a breakpoint is set by the large red dot next to the line of source code, as shown in Figure 5.7.

Step Debugger Tutorial Part II

1. Your cursor (the yellow arrow) should be pointing to the first line of the main program, which starts with the keyword *bool*. If it's not, press **F11** to **Step Into** the program.
2. Press the **F10** key and the cursor will **Step Over** to the next line, *while*.
3. The line *bool* has now been executed.
4. The current line, **while**, is now waiting to be executed. Press **F10** again.
5. The cursor jumps to the last line of the entire program. This is a major clue as to the first logic error in the program.
6. Since the line **while** seems to be the last line executed, let's set a breakpoint there.

Figure 5.6
The Breakpoint
Menu

✂	Cut
🗐	Copy
📋	Paste
	Open File
🖑	Insert Breakpoint
🖑	New Breakpoint...
👓	Add Watch
👓	QuickWatch...
⇨	Show Next Statement
→▣	Run To Cursor
🤸	Set Next Statement
🔡	Go To Disassembly
	Add Task List Shortcut
🔲	List Members
🔲	Parameter Info
A⁺	Complete Word
🔲	Quick Info

Figure 5.7
The Breakpoint
Indicator

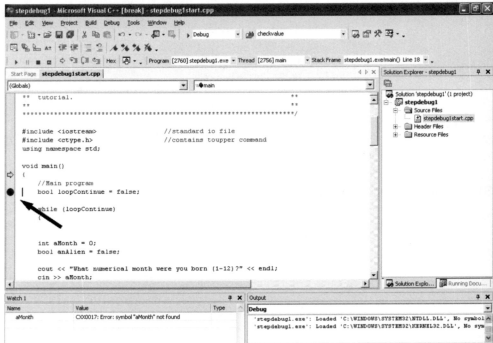

7. Right-click on the line **while** and choose **Insert Breakpoint** (see Figure 5.8).

Figure 5.8
Inserting a
Breakpoint

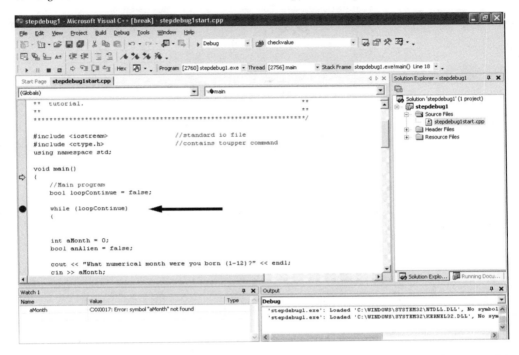

8. The breakpoint will cause the debugger to stop here when the program runs. We need to restart the program first however. Open the **Debug** menu and choose **Restart**, as shown in Figure 5.9.

Figure 5.9
Restarting the
Program

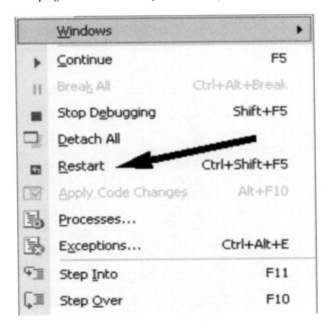

9. The yellow cursor will now return to the first line of the main program and you can now just hit **F5** (**Continue**) to jump down to the breakpoint. Press **F5**.

10. This is a loop call for a while loop that is controlled by the value of the Boolean, `loopContinue`. If the Boolean is true, then the loop runs or continues to run. If the Boolean is false, the loop stops. Check the value of the Boolean by setting up a watch on this variable. This is done using the **Watch** window pane in the lower-left corner. You can add the variable `loopContinue` to the **Watch** pane by simply typing its name on the first line, as shown in Figure 5.10. The `loopContinue` variable automatically appears on the Auto tab and on the Locals tab (since it is in the local scope) so you may want to check it without adding a permanent watch.

Figure 5.10
The Watch Pane

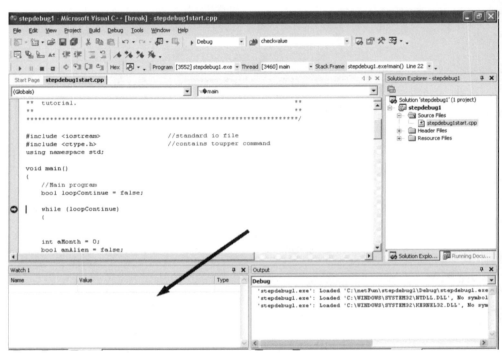

11. This will now "watch" the variable's value while the program runs. Note that its current value is 0, false. This tells the programmer the loop will never run.

12. The programmer must then decide why the value is false. If you look at the variable's initialization on the `bool` line, you will see that it is set to false—an obvious error that resulted in a bizarre outcome. Change the value of the initialization of `loopContinue` to `true`, as shown in Figure 5.11.

13. This will require you to resave the program and recompile. All this can be accomplished using the menus as you have learned earlier: **Stop Debugging** (**Shift-F5**) and then recompile (**Debug**, **Build Solution**).

14. Now, you should run the program again and see what happens.

15. The program will ask you for the month you were born (see Figure 5.12). Just for example, use September. Type the number **9** and press **Return**.

16. You should see the Message, `Sapphire is your birthstone!` and be offered the option to continue, as shown in Figure 5.13. Choose **y** and press **Return**.

Figure 5.11
Changing a
value

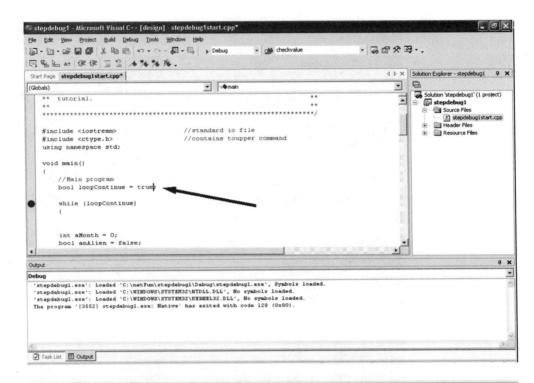

Figure 5.12
Enter the
Number 9

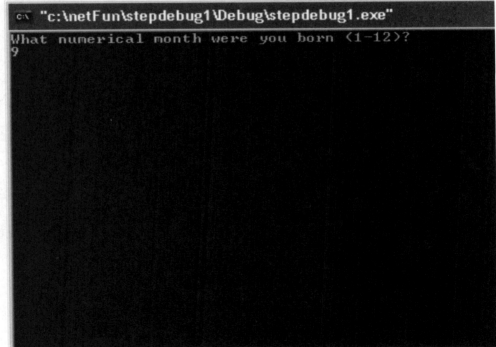

Figure 5.13
The Successful
Run

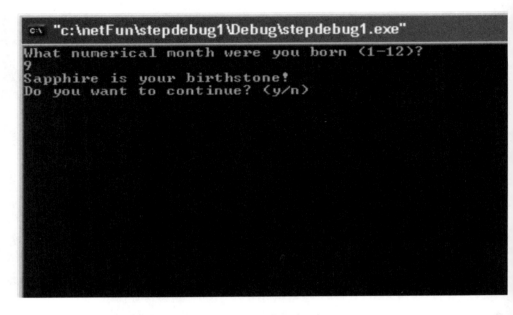

Figure 5.14
The Problem
with October

Program Testing

Commercial programs are tested thousands of times by different people to attempt to determine if any errors exist. Imagine your embarrassment when your program requires the release of a patch. Despite programmers' desire to release error-free code, problems that were never tested may slip through.

Using test data is one approach to determining where errors exist. In the tutorial so far, we have done what is called "sampling," which is testing some of the functionality of the program but not all. It is often the case with commercial products that not all the potential problems can be tested, given the deadlines and desires of the company. Thus, sampling may be used with the assumption that if 50 percent (or some other percentage) of the functions work, all the rest will probably work.

If possible, however, companies would prefer exhaustive, or "population," testing. This means that very possible option is tested before the program is released. This may take a great deal of time, but it will reduce the number of patches needed later.

Step Debugging Tutorial Part III

Our program so far seems to work with our eight percent sample (1/12). Let's test the program exhaustively.

1. If your program is still running from Part II just continue, otherwise execute your program again.
2. Work through the entire numerical sequence (1-12) for all the birthstones and see if you find any anomalies.
3. Note that 10 doesn't work (see Figure 5.14). It looks like people born in October are out of luck with this program.
4. There must be an error somewhere in the source code causing a problem. Again, the Step Debugger can help. Choose **n** to stop your program and start the debugger with **Step Into**.
5. Since everything seems to work until the program decides on the month, let's set a breakpoint at the beginning of the `switch` statement where the decisions are made. You may want to remove the breakpoint on the while line since the `while` loop seems OK at this point (see Figure 5.15).
6. Now you can run the program down to the breakpoint. Click the **Debug, Continue** menu item (or press **F5**) to run down to the breakpoint.
7. Answer the questions that appear in the program's DOS window. Since we are interested in October, enter **10** and press **Return** when the window appears (see Figure 5.16).
8. The program will stop at the breakpoint you set and now we can step through. Let's verify the variable by checking the **quickwatch** (or you can add it to the watch pane as in Part II).
9. Hold down the left mouse button and drag over the variable. This will select the variable `aMonth`, as shown in Figure 5.17.

Figure 5.15
Inserting and
Removing
Breakpoints
Again

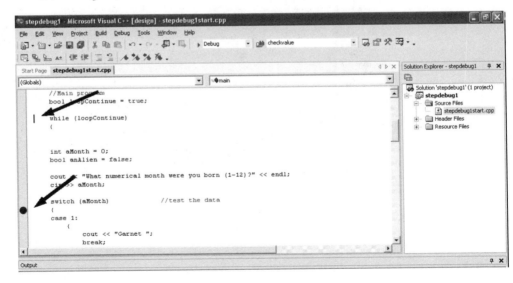

Figure 5.16
The DOS
Window Again

Figure 5.17
Selecting a
Variable with the
Mouse

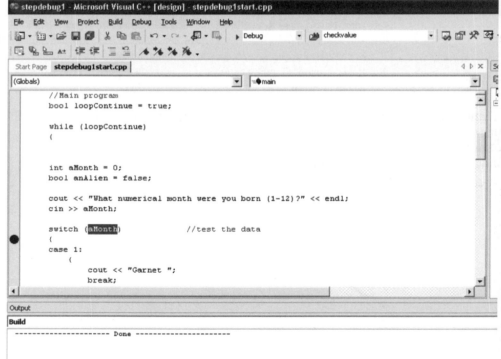

gure 5.18
uickWatch

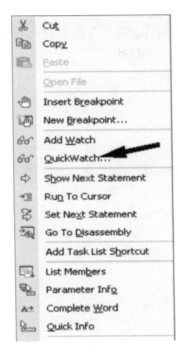

	Cut
	Copy
	Paste
	Open File
	Insert Breakpoint
	New Breakpoint...
	Add Watch
	QuickWatch...
	Show Next Statement
	Run To Cursor
	Set Next Statement
	Go To Disassembly
	Add Task List Shortcut
	List Members
	Parameter Info
	Complete Word
	Quick Info

10. Now, right-click the mouse and a menu appears. Choose **QuickWatch** on the menu, as shown in Figure 5.18.
11. You will see the **QuickWatch** pane appear (see Figure 5.19).

Figure 5.19
The QuickWatch
Pane

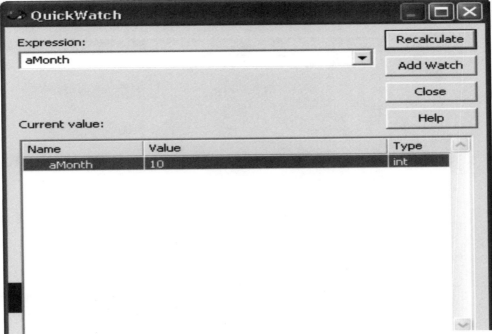

QuickWatch

Expression:

aMonth

Recalculate
Add Watch
Close
Help

Current value:

Name	Value	Type
aMonth	10	int

Figure 5.20
The Variable
Value

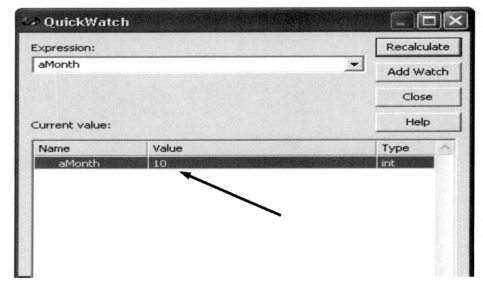

12. If you look at the value of the variable as shown in Figure 5.20, you see it is "10," which is what you presumed it to be. This means the error is somewhere else, but at least we know the variable was input correctly.

13. Although the variable is correct on this line, something could change it, so let's add it to the **Watch** pane to keep an eye on it as the program runs. Click the **Add Watch** button (see Figure 5.20) on the **QuickWatch** pane.

14. aMonth will then appear in the **Watch** pane in the left-hand corner of the screen, as shown in Figure 5.21. Press the **Close** button on the **QuickWatch** pane.

Figure 5.21
The Watch Pane

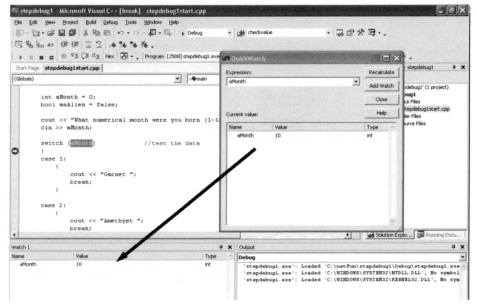

Figure 5.22
The Default
Section of the
Program

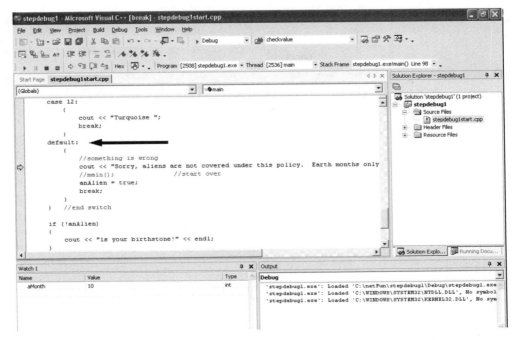

15. Now, let's step a line at a time using **Step Over** (**F10**) and see what happens. Press **F10**.
16. The program jumps to the `default` section of the choices, as shown in Figure 5.22.
17. That would imply that the `10` section got skipped. Move up and look at the line for the `10` options above, as shown in Figure 5.23.

Figure 5.23
The 10 Section

```
case 19:
    {
        cout << "Opal ";
        break;
    }
case 11:
    {
        cout << "Topaz ";
        break;
    }
case 12:
    {
        cout << "Turquoise ";
```

18. Hmmm, it's set to 19, as Figure 5.23 illustrates. Perhaps the programmer accidentally typed 9 instead of 0 (they are close together on the keyboard).
19. Correct the error by deleting the 9 and replacing it with a 0 (see Figure 5.24).

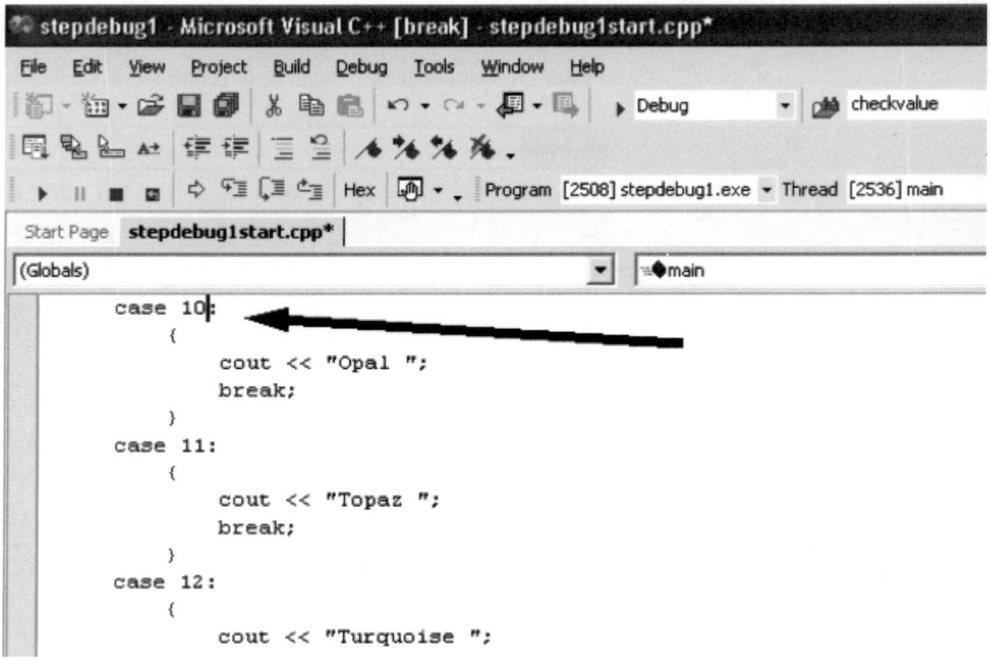

Figure 5.24
Replace the 9 with a 0

20. **Save** and **Recompile** using the menus or F keys.
21. You should again get the error-free compile.

This completes the tutorial on the **Step Debugger**. This is a powerful tool that will help you in both testing and debugging logic errors.

Chapter 5 Exercises

1. Use the Step Debugger to work through the logic problems in **stepdebug2**, which is on your disk and also on the Website.

2. Use the Step Debugger to work through the logic problems in **stepdebug3**, which is on your disk and also on the Website.